Expecting It All

www.mascotbooks.com

Expecting It All: More Time, Money, Energy, and Space for Mothers

Note from the author on AI use: The words in these pages are entirely my own. The only exceptions are two pull quotes, for which I consulted ChatGPT to rephrase my own writing into shorter takeaways. I did so with the intention of bringing you a more enjoyable reading experience.

For more information, please contact:
Mascot Books, an imprint of Amplify Publishing Group
620 Herndon Parkway, Suite 220
Herndon, VA 20170
info@amplifypublishing.com

Library of Congress Control Number: 2024916408

CPSIA Code: PRV1024A

ISBN-13: 979-8-89138-116-2

Printed in the United States

To my husband and daughter—
the love and joy of my world.

Special thanks to Whitney McGruder—
I couldn't have done this without you.

Expecting It All

More Time, Money, Energy, and Space for Mothers

JANET BRUINS

CONTENTS

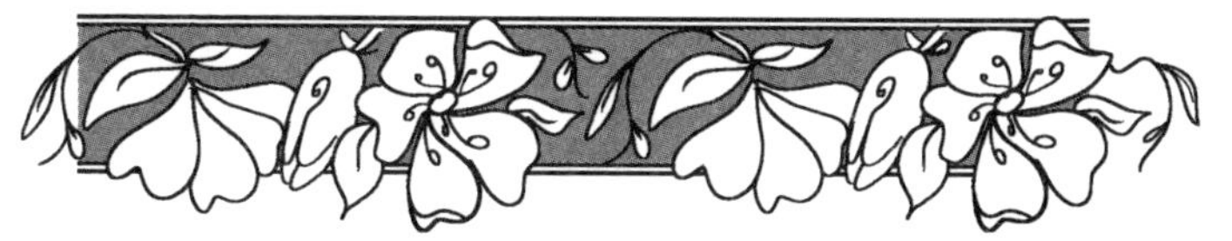

Prologue

A few months after my daughter was born, I put on my sneakers to take a walk. There is a trail just behind my house. Paved and lined with mature trees, the path turns each stroll into pure pleasure. One can hear songbirds, cicadas, and the croaking of frogs while walking on the path. The shade reduces the outdoor temperature by ten degrees. And when there is a breeze, you can feel it with all of your senses as the wind rustles the leaves and the sun creates dancing shapes on the pavement.

I walked for only fifteen minutes and decided to turn around to head back home. Despite the beautiful surroundings, I suddenly felt drained and exhausted. This was when I found that I couldn't move. It hit me that I was mentally exhausted, drained to the point that I couldn't bring myself to repeatedly lift one foot in front of another.

We waited to have a baby.

I built my career. After graduating with a STEM degree, I worked as an engineer for over ten years. There were stretches of weeks where I was at the job site for over twelve hours every day. I was frugal. Twenty percent of my income went into savings and retirement. I fell in love and married a man who is loving, supportive, and, just as importantly, knows how to do dishes.

We planned for this baby, making sure we were as ready as possible before starting a family.

Even though I wasn't always a happy pregnant lady, I thought everything was going alright. I had an obstetrician who was invested in our well-being. I had five weeks of short-term disability pay from my insurance for recovery after giving birth. My sister lived close by, and so did my in-laws. I read pregnancy books and thought about names for the baby.

I did everything I could but still ended up stranded in the middle of the trail, on a beautiful day less than a quarter mile from my own home, and couldn't move my body to get back. I wasn't angry or bitter. It was just a vague sense of confusion on how to get back home. I didn't have my phone with me, and there was no one around. Even if someone was walking past, it would have been difficult to explain that I had dipped into postpartum depression unexpectedly and was struggling to get home.

So, I summoned whatever emotional strength I hadn't already tapped into to drag myself back so I could be in time to feed my baby and prepare to return to the office after my five-week maternity leave was up.

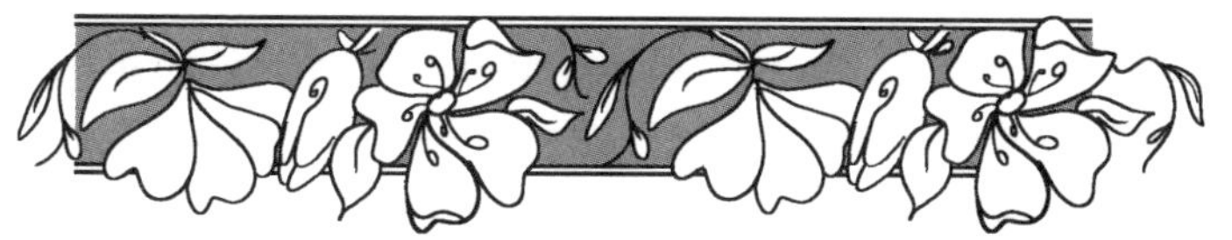

CHAPTER 1

It's OK to Expect It All

In 2019, I met with a colleague at a coffee shop near my office. I was pregnant with my daughter and busy preparing for my maternity leave. She had just given birth to her son and was returning to work after taking leave of her own. I remembered her being cheerful and energetic, which really irked me.

Everything irked me back then. A pregnant belly was like an open invitation for strangers to approach and converse with me. I got into an argument with a waiter for ordering sashimi—the waiter lectured me that raw fish is bad for my unborn child. I quipped back that if he and I were both doing our jobs, then my body would take care of any harmful substance from two ounces of fish, and he would take my order and serve me the food. In the end, I didn't eat anything, but added raw fish to my growing list of pregnancy taboos.

Being pregnant and in a coffee shop made me just as uneasy as that brief foray at the sushi bar. I scanned the room, making sure no one was thinking of having a go at me for drinking coffee before returning to the conundrum at hand. My colleague was obviously looking for some pleasant company, but all I wanted to do was to scream at her, "You're a mom now and will never be able to own nice things or travel anywhere other than visiting your in-laws. All your fun friends will desert you and be replaced by other moms who only talk about their kids. The word 'brunch' will forever disappear from your vocabulary. You'll find out that the man you married is incapable of changing diapers. The only sentence you'll contribute to meetings will be 'I need to go pick up my kids . . .' and, after all of that, you will think of yourself as a terrible mother to a bunch of ungrateful brats!"

That was my prepartum depression talking. I didn't have a child until I was thirty-nine. A large part of the delay was because my hunt for a partner took longer than expected. I also felt I had to achieve and experience everything before having a child. After all, it's all about your child after giving birth, isn't it?

I lived most of my adult life with anxiety about becoming a mother. To start, there are the potential effects of pregnancy: I may or may not be hit with moodiness, bloating, constipation, food craving or aversion, and of course, the well-known morning sickness, which I was also told is not actually confined to just mornings. Then there is the childbirth process, which can turn into a major surgery, as over 30 percent of women in America receive a six-inch incision in their abdomen by a surgeon's scalpel.[1]

Finally, there is the brain alteration after the arrival of my bundle of joy. Researchers from the University of Denver, University of Iowa, and the University of Michigan looked into the change in neuroplasticity across the postpartum period. They concluded that regardless of the individual differences, mothers' brains are changed to support mother-infant relationships.[2] Like it or not, one will have "mommy brain" after giving birth—evolution demands so. Some women even described having a new heart after their child arrived. It sounded like alien abduction, except for it being voluntary and I was standing in line, ready for my own life alteration.

After that day at the coffee shop with my colleague, I gave birth to my baby girl and promptly started to live out my self-fulfilling prophecies. I couldn't help it. I didn't know any better.

The most repeated advice I received from books was "sleep when the baby sleeps." Some days I did just that, but most days I didn't feel like sleeping for twenty hours within a twenty-four-hour period. The better advice was from my sister-in-law, who told me to choose a good show to binge-watch while breastfeeding. I ended up finishing ten seasons of *Grey's Anatomy* and Beyoncé's *Homecoming* documentary the moment it aired on Netflix (temporarily marking me as one of the most in-the-know Queen Bey fans). If you had told me new mothers benefit from line dancing, I would have added "best boots for dancing" along with other questions I googled at 2:00 a.m. (Most of those questions are variations of "is [fill in the blank about my baby] normal?")

My husband, Jeff, and I planned our pregnancy and the childbirth with a precision that can only be attributed to a new couple's naivety. I still remember the immense joy I felt when I first knew I was pregnant. My little darling was to be born in the year of the Golden Pig.[3] This auspicious beginning foretold comfort and wealth for the entirety of my child's life. Within a year of her birth, a virus killed my ambitions of country-hopping across the planet. The economy had shuttered in response, and my golden piggy blew out the candle on a homemade cupcake in front of a camera so her relatives could cheer from a safe distance. Life seldom goes according to plan.

Nine months later, I was grasping at straws trying to construct a new mental image where I would thrive along with my baby, but with a newborn changing in the blink of an eye, my husband and I were struggling to build any routines that we could stick to. Planning our future seemed both pointless and insurmountable. Instead, I gave up on myself and fully accepted the idea that I should devote all thoughts and energy to caring for my daughter. She was right there, ready for me to revolve my life around. My future was unknown. The clearest goalpost was eighteen years in the future when she would go off to college.

When my daughter Rosie turned two, my depression lifted. It was like someone finally noticed me in the brain pain waiting room, said "What are you still doing here?", opened the door, and shoved me out. We have known about mental illnesses related to childbirth for as long as women started having children. The signs of being tired, feeling anxious, irritable, overwhelmed, or even guilty and worthless appear in one out of five new moms.[4] About half of women experience minor "baby blues" that last less than two weeks.[5] The rest of us, myself included, are under the storm clouds for significantly longer.

There are still debates on the best time to detect and treat women experiencing postpartum depression. Six to twelve months?[6] Perhaps two years?[7] Researchers are still investigating the best ways to intervene, but none of that would have mattered for me anyway since the only doctor's office I was visiting was the pediatrician's for Rosie's checkup.

I worked on reclaiming a life for myself. It was not easy, like nobody expected I would want anything for myself besides a happy and healthy child.

After shaking my postpartum depression funk, I spoke to my manager regarding career advancement. He looked at me with interest and consternation, as if there was nothing in the cards for me and it would take both him and me some work to get me to the next career level.

While pregnant, I confidently told him that I was all set. No promotions for me, thank you very much. There is a time to pursue a career and a time to take care of family. Any sensible modern-day woman knows that you can't have it all, at least not at the same time. I thought I was wise to set his expectations low in case he had it in his head that I would give up the joy and comfort of my own family just to prioritize career advancement.

Honestly, I was lucky he didn't laugh me out of the room. For the past two years I felt I did nothing other than smile at Rosie's baby picture at work. And perhaps walking laps between the printer and my desk to get my 10,000 steps in each day.

After my manager performed the miracle of getting me back on the career ladder (this included adding my name to the watchlist for potential promotion and me working to earn that promotion), and thereby completing some of the requirements for sainthood, I looked around for other areas of my life to improve. And there, I was at a loss again. Now that I've collected the bingo chips of family and career, already deemed impossible or overreaching by many, would it be too much for me to expect more?

It is not too much. It is not too much for a mother to ask for her own mental happiness and physical well-being. It is not too much for a mother to indulge in hobbies that bring her joy. It is not too much for a mother to desire lifelong learning that does not involve learning to cook and clean better. And it is not too much for her to ask for the world to see her as more than just a caregiver. But first she must see herself as more. She has to expect it all from herself and the world.

This is a book for mothers, but it is not meant to give parenting advice. I often tell mothers that your children won the lottery the minute they were born because they have you as their mother and role model. This book is also not about policy change. There are many people who are speaking up for changes. There are many people who are already creating change. While I provide extensive research for this book, I have sought out information that can help other mothers on an individual level. I recommend looking to local organizations and activists for further information on how to create change on a community level.

This book is about you. I want you to use the same lens you use when you look at your child and gaze upon yourself. I hope you discover that you are beautiful, whole, and deserving. Too often women use a traditional yardstick to measure themselves: is my child deemed exceptional by others, am I getting recognized and promoted at work, did I lose my pregnancy weight, and am I getting lots of attention when I post about my life on social media?

If you've gone through pregnancy, delivery, or any other trauma, I want to help you find ways to heal yourself.

In this book, I also want to provide you with practical advice on how you can get more resources for yourself. The issuc I hear from many mothers is that they have given themselves away. There is barely enough fuel for them to care for others, let alone anything remaining to lift themselves up. Therefore, I want to provide tips on how you can gain more time, money, energy, and space for yourself.

Please remember: what you gain, you keep for yourself. My hope is that this will be a starting point for you to grow into the happiness I desire for you.

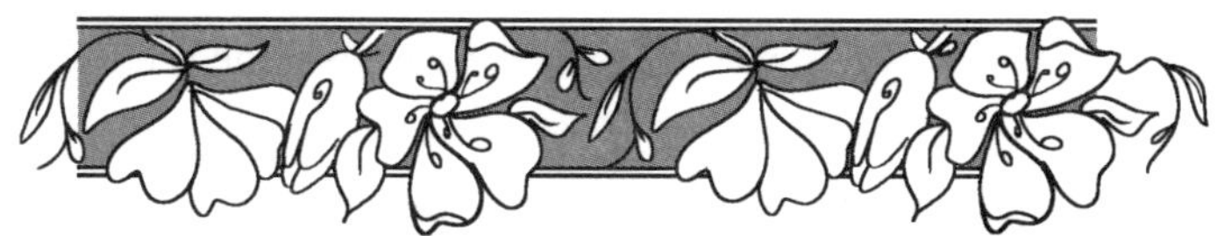

CHAPTER 2

On the Fence about Motherhood

Winston Churchill advised having four children: "one to reproduce your [partner], one to reproduce yourself, one for the increase in population, and one in case of accident."[1] The Churchills ended up having five children, so perhaps the lesson here is to not make pronouncements on how many kids other people should have.

While the decision to become a mother is yours, truly and absolutely, I wanted to devote a portion of this book to help you figure out if you would like playing the role of mom and what comes with the territory.

Should I Have Kids? If So, How Many?

In February 2003, I started my first full-time job. That was also around the time when I started wondering whether I wanted to be a mother.

I spent about fifteen years of my life thinking about the motherhood question. It came from uncertainties: where I would live, who I would marry, how much we could earn, when I want to add a kid into the mix, whether that will still be my decision or would that be made for me due to infertility or the overturn of *Roe v. Wade*.

In the beginning, I thought four kids was a good number, just shy of a van-full. I imagined raising these kids with a farmer/carpenter—someone earthy who enjoys soups (which is the only thing I could really make). I was living in the Midwest and there was an abundance of ingredients to make that life happen (e.g., vans, farmers, carpenters, and lands and woods for my farmer/carpenter to stay busy with).

But when I spent a lot of time in Manhattan, I didn't want children. Instead, I wanted to go to parties, museums, thrift stores, bars, and live partially out of LaGuardia airport as I traveled the world.

After moving to Northern Virginia, I thought I should at least have one child. After all, someone should enjoy the good schools my tax dollars were paying for. I wanted a man with plenty of hobbies so we wouldn't run out of things to do during government shutdowns. Someone with strong political opinions, ideas on how to fix the Supreme Court, and the social intelligence to know when to keep those thoughts to himself. Most importantly, I wanted someone to share the cost of living with and perhaps think I'm swell enough to settle down for the long haul.

While it would have been helpful if someone sat me down and explained the motherhood transformation, it probably wouldn't have made a difference in terms of the amount of time I spent considering this question.

Am I Ready to Have Kids?
Will I Regret Having Kids?

From personal experience and from observing women around me, the factors in deciding whether to have kids include age, presence of partner, health, fertility, and wealth, roughly in that order.

After a certain age, if there is a suitable partner and the woman is healthy, the thought of having a child most likely crosses her mind. The thought of fertility usually comes after trying to conceive for a certain period, and while everyone worries about the expense of raising a child, in the end that doesn't always hold people back from having children.

Jeff works with a younger crowd; most of them do not have kids yet. When asked about when someone can know if they're ready to have kids, he gives this answer: children tend to magnify everything in life. Your problems will magnify, and so will the joyful moments of your life. While it's true that you'll never be at a point in life where you're absolutely ready to have kids, you're probably more prepared than you think if you have steady work, a steady home, and a steady partner.

Scott Galloway, co-host of the podcast *Pivot*, puts it well:

"[If] you're in a loving, secure relationship and economically viable, [then] you're quite frankly in central casting to have kids.[2] Note that neither Scott nor I believe you need to be in a traditional husband and wife relationship to count, although it's probably a good idea to have a committed co-parent, whether that's a spouse, a partner, a grandparent, or even a daycare center.

To say that no mother ever regrets having children—not even a passing thought—is disingenuous. I remember within the first week of bringing Rosie home I was horrified at what I had done—I've had a baby, and I will never stop worrying about her for the rest of my life. Something as precious as my organs had come out of me, and now, I couldn't put it back. I thought it was as dumb of a decision as deciding to carry my heart around on the outside.

Then there were the times when I was spiraling into depression and mourned deeply for the places I might never go because of my child. But if I examined those feelings at the time, it was not regret. They were dark and gloomy, with a large amount of irritation and incredible sadness. But it wasn't regret.

As Rosie grew and began communicating with me (around the age of two), I found my positive feelings toward her shot up, and my negative feelings dissipated. Aside from being the most adorable little beanie that's ever lived, I think my positivity has a lot to do with the fact that Rosie is an easy

Children tend to magnify everything in life—your best days become better, but your worst problems are compounded as well.

child. She had some sleeping problems (for the first three years of her life, Jeff and I never had an entire week where we didn't have to wake up multiple times a night to put her back to bed). She's still somewhat of a picky eater (there were a few months where the only food she would eat consistently was canned chicken noodle soup). Other than that, she has few tantrums and gives great hugs.

In that respect, Jeff and I are very lucky. I don't have the delusion that Rosie's good behaviors were solely due to good parenting on our part. From the books I've read and talking to teachers and mothers with multiple kids, I know that you get all kinds.

Pregnancy Changes Everything—Positively and Negatively

At a dinner party, I heard about a woman who really lucked out during her pregnancy. Normally gluten-intolerant, she found that somehow her body was happily accepting doughy-carb-heavy goodness when she was carrying her baby. She spent most of her nine months joyfully indulging in pizzas and pastas.

Most of us are not that lucky. On average, 70 to 80 percent of women will experience what is commonly referred to as "morning sickness."[3]

Doctors, with their love of acronyms, refer to this symptom as "nausea and vomiting in pregnancy" or NVP. A very bad case of nausea and vomiting is called HG, or hyperemesis gravidarum. Medically speaking, while both are awful, HG may be dangerous to mother and baby if left untreated.

If you are less than thirty-five years old and on your first pregnancy, your obstetrician will call you young and primigravida (i.e., first pregnancy). You have a greater chance of throwing up during your first trimester, so definitely prepare yourself. On top of that, if you are Caucasian and carrying twins, then you are primigravida with multiple gestation (which means carrying twins), so for sure expect the normal unpleasantness of pregnancy. Almost 90 percent of women carrying more than one baby reported NVP during the first trimester. If you're over thirty-five and your obstetrician calls you geriatric, then you are entitled to feel offended and nauseous.

While women get pregnant, have babies, raise families, and kick butt in the workplace all the time, you want to be prepared for your specific case of the unknown symptoms during pregnancy. Although HG is rare (occurring less than 2 percent of the time), there is a possibility that just normal pregnancy symptoms will affect your performance on the job. Even if you weather through the first twenty weeks of pregnancy, after which morning sickness tends to subside, there may still be other complications that will require you to take time off.

Other complications include gestational diabetes (diabetes during pregnancy) which occurs about 3 to 8 percent of the time, placenta previa (complications with the placenta) occurs about 0.5 percent of the time, and preeclampsia (high blood pressure during pregnancy) occurs about 5 to 8 percent of the time.[4, 5, 6] In short, pregnancy is a big change, and we just don't know how other parts of your body will respond.

Pregnancy is the first time mothers weigh their well-being against their babies. In other words, this is the first of a million times when you will be sacrificing for your child. It may be easy to believe that anything that maximizes the chance of your baby's well-being is always worth sacrificing for. But there are times that the risk to your pregnancy is so miniscule that it really doesn't make sense to change your lifestyle.

Take coffee as an example. Caffeine is a stimulant, therefore there is a chance that drinking coffee may not be good for your baby. But we don't actually know whether this is true, specifically to you and your baby, and, if so, by how much.

This is why mothers agonize over whether they should do something for themselves or go without for the benefit of their child. While the joy of coffee may be small, small things add up. The questionable damage to your child is both unknown in chance and quantity.

You have to make this choice.

For example, maybe you question whether your current medication would be harmful to the fetus. If you're on a certain medication, it is because you need it. It is a confirmed fact that the drug indeed benefits you. When you and your doctor are considering that medication's effect on the baby, you are trying

Prioritizing your own well-being can benefit both mother and child more than sacrificing indiscriminately on their behalf.

to answer two questions: What is the chance it will harm the baby and by how much?

I want to take a minute here to talk about anti-depression and anti-anxiety meditations. If you are on these types of medication prior to pregnancy and are thinking that you should go off them for the wellness of your baby, please make sure you are making a well-informed decision. I recommend seeing a psychiatrist in addition to your obstetrician to get a full understanding of your medication's potential impact on pregnancy.

Your obstetrician (OB) is there to see that you have a healthy pregnancy and delivery. Your psychiatrist's job is to ensure your mental well-being under any circumstances. A study shows that the risk of relapse into depression is as high as 68 percent when women go off their medications, and depression is not a state in which you want to start your journey of motherhood.[7]

Why Become a Parent?

"You're not selling me on this parenting thing."

Jeff was at his company's watering hole, an all-in-one cafe/bar located in the same building as his office. We were having a conversation with his colleagues on what it was like to be a parent.

Jeff thought for a minute and responded. "Say you have a good friend, and you learned that he's never seen a sunset before. Change 'sunset' into literally anything. This person doesn't know about rainbows, or baseball, or Harry Potter. They get to see it for the first time, and you get to see them seeing it for the first time."

He continued, "They get to learn about rocks, mud, and sand. You bring them to the beach, and they just want to grab a handful of sand and put it in their mouth. And, depending on what type of parent you are, you either jump in and shout 'no, no, no!' or you sit back and let it happen. *That* is the amazing thing about being a parent."

I smiled when Jeff recounted this story. I've seen him feeling frustrated, defeated, and exhausted when caring for Rosie, but none of that ever dampens the excitement for him. The other day, after returning from the grocery store, I saw him so giddy he seemed ready to burst because he had bought some hot cocoa and was going to introduce that to Rosie for the first time (if she was a good eater and finished her dinner, of course).

My father sometimes talks about scarcity in his childhood. He recounted seeing a neighbor boy eating an orange and thinking to himself, "哇! He gets to eat a whole orange all by himself! An entire orange! No sharing!" Guess what we never lacked in our house when I was growing up? Oranges.

Similar to my father, I find myself looking for ways to provide Rosie with things I lacked when growing up.

I was raised in Taiwan at a time when corporal punishment was common in school. When I was in the third and fourth grade, I had a homeschool teacher who used the stick freely as a way to scare kids from getting bad grades.

Now that I have a child, it brings me deep cathartic joy selecting Rosie's daycare and speaking with each of her teachers. This act of caring for my child healed the wounds I didn't know I had. Every day when I picked her up at daycare, she would run toward me, happy and excited to tell me what she did that day. I would hug her as tightly as she would let me, and I hear the child within myself say to me, "You did good."

Why become a parent? Becoming a parent has changed the way I look at the world, has helped me heal parts of myself I didn't know needed to be healed, and has made me grow as a person. While not everyone will decide to become a parent, if you need a reason, just know that along with the bad comes even more good.

Not everyone chooses parenthood, but for those seeking a reason, know this: amidst challenges await abundant joys.

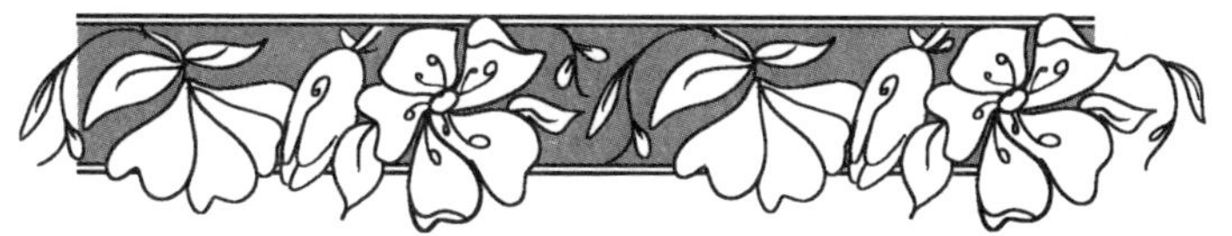

CHAPTER 3

The Craft of Dreamweaving

Chasing your dream is scary.

I used to have a detailed pro versus con list for every potential endeavor, where I carefully listed and calculated each risk before maybe considering taking the leap. My biggest concern usually was the fear of looking like a fool, followed by "What if it doesn't work?" which was then closely followed by "What if it does work and I find that's not what I wanted after all?"

It was difficult to move forward under that mindset.

Now, as a mother, I'm taking more chances than before.

I'm putting in all this work raising my daughter, making sure she grows up big and strong, and happy, grounded, confident, humble, kind, and curious . . . it would be a shame if she doesn't do anything with these positive qualities. Therefore, I am choosing to do more with my life first so she can grow up learning that dreams are nothing to fear.

Here is a letter to my daughter I'd like to share with you:

Dear Rosie,

I am writing this letter to you because one day I hope you will have the joy of knowing that you can truly achieve everything your heart desires.

You were born into a world of abundance. Not only are you surrounded with endless material and opportunities, your father and I did our best to raise you with a growth mindset. However, there will be things you want that will test your limits. You won't know it at the time, but the struggle will be the best part of the process. I don't want you to be flawless. I want you to experience the crucible (at least once in your life) to burn away any doubt you may have of your abilities.

While there are strategies and steps to reach every dream, the secret ingredient to success is faith. Don't limit yourself in what you wish for. You have a good and strong heart—you will want the best for yourself, the people you love, and the world you live in. Do not settle for less.

Now go. Create the world you dreamed of and live the life you want.

Love - Mom

After Rosie was born, I was in constant low-grade existential crisis mode for almost two years. I found motherhood confusing at first because so much of my identity was tied to my accomplishments, and a baby really slowed me down. Am I still a go-getter when I walk around in my pajamas all day? Can I still consider myself put-together when washing my hair is a high bar? Can I still call myself a bad bitch when I have to spell out b-i-t-c-h because little ears are listening?

The sense of identity loss after childbirth can really take a toll. Looking back, it was the major reason that landed me in postnatal depression. In my twenties and early thirties, pushing myself to the limit was my jam. For about a year, I would wrap up my nine-to-five day job as an engineer, then pick up a couple shifts a week as a cook at a local restaurant. I also picked up a couple of graduate degrees in the evenings this way. Hustling felt like the only way I could get to where I wanted to go in life.

When my baby came along, it took everything I had just to keep my head above water. Her needs were constant and unrelenting. She needed to be fed, cleaned, and entertained. Even when I wasn't directly caring for her, my mind was wholly occupied with finding a solution to the latest childcare challenge.

I kept thinking to myself, *After this hurdle, surely I will have more time for myself.*

But the hurdles just kept coming.

For the first few months, I dealt with a newborn's needs every two to four hours around the clock. Then I tried to get

Rosie to sleep through the night and switch her to eating solids. Eventually, she became more mobile, and I had to watch her movement every second to make sure she wouldn't randomly fall over and crack her head open. Then, back to worrying about what she eats—I wondered whether it was possible to grow a child on just pizza and mac-and-cheese.

Once, I asked a male colleague of mine how he was able to solve a particularly thorny problem at work. He told me earnestly that he would sit quietly and mentally walk through each step of the problem to reach a solution.

His answer highlighted the gap between myself and those I worked with. It was rather discouraging since quiet moments were hard to come by as a mother. And when they did come, all my mental energy was still channeled into figuring out how to feed my daughter more vegetables.

While drowning in self-doubt, I asked myself why I was hustling during my pre-Rosie days. What was I trying to prove, and where was I trying to go?

Throughout high school and college, I was loading up as much work as possible to get ahead and move on to the next level. I needed a solid GPA, high marks in every math and science assignment, and an extracurricular activity or two to get into engineering school. In engineering school, I had to attend lectures and office hours, spend countless hours in the lab, participate in organizations, and find internships to get enough on a résumé to land my first job.

Even after getting a few years of work experience under my belt, I was still doing the same thing—overloading my plate to exhaustion. While this was doable, even fun in a challenging way, having a child made me realize not everything can be solved or improved upon by my sheer willpower.

One day when I was picking up Rosie from daycare, she excitedly pointed at the sunset and yelled, "Mommy! Look at the *more-then* lights!" Somewhere she heard the term "northern lights," decided it must be related to sunsets, and came up with her own version of the words.

Somehow, she had grown into this crazy, adorable, and laughably silly child, mostly on her own. Had she been shaped entirely through my anxiety and determination, she probably would have become a killjoy, fuddy-duddy instead.

This realization helped me shift the time horizon in my mind. Caring for my child does not need to be the all-consuming activity I had made it out to be. I, too, can sit quietly (with the help of a babysitter) and spend my time and mental energy on myself.

Until Rosie turns into a teenager and is later lawfully allowed to fly the coop to pursue her own dream, I should take some time to focus on myself and my dreams.

Making Things Happen

I was on the rooftop at 1700 K Street NW, in the business district of Washington, DC. The small space was packed, mostly with businessmen and women coming directly from work. There was a variety of wine being offered at one station, and another station was loaded with appetizers and desserts.

My friend ‘Iolani saw me walking into the room. She got up from her stool where she was chatting with a small group of people and walked over to give me a hug. I immediately remembered how tall she was. As I reacquainted myself with old friends after the pandemic, I was sometimes shocked to be reminded that they were more than just faces on my computer screen.

The two of us were at a panel event. She was invited to speak about her experience of writing a children’s book while also parenting two young children. I watched while she walked to the front of the room and took her place with the other panelists. We went to school together. ‘Iolani is always so warm and graceful that one can completely forget the fact that she is towering over you.

In 2018, ‘Iolani was pregnant and preparing for her maternity leave. Her husband’s job was going to take him to Thailand for a stint. By any other measure, this would seem like terrible timing—to temporarily lose a partner during the key time of bonding with a new baby. ‘Iolani, however, thought differently.

“Why don’t we just all go?” she explained her reasoning. “There’s nothing holding us back—no job I have to go to.”

She was going to be out on maternity leave and have time to herself without interruption, which really appealed to her.

This wasn't going to be her first time in Thailand. 'Iolani had been on a solo trip to Bangkok before. She also did tons of research online before leaving. For example, she learned that there are a very limited number of airplane seats with bassinets on every plane, and she was able to book one of them early and avoid sitting with her infant on her lap for the whole trip.

She also knew from her experience that it would be difficult to navigate Bangkok with a stroller. From her research online, she found that there are high-quality diapers available in Thailand (imported from Japan), and that saved her a lot of space from packing.

People around her were more skeptical.

"Everyone thought that we were insane," recalled 'Iolani. "'What if [the baby] gets sick? Where are you going to get diapers? What if you need baby formula?' I mean . . . I was thrown every question."

'Iolani already had confidence in her abilities. And her confidence didn't waiver even though she was going through a major change of looking after both herself and her newborn.

"You have to go with your intuition and your gut. If I just listened to everyone else and just stayed home, I wouldn't have taken this journey."

Contrasting with my own experience, I spent my maternity leave at home. Well, of course I was going to—no sane person would have done anything differently. Knowing that I would be in a familiar environment, I did not do much to prepare. I thought that when the time came, I would just devote time to nursing and sleeping.

When my baby came, I completely lost myself without even realizing that was possible. I was like a tourist: map in one hand, camera in another, heading toward a popular destination. When I got there, it was a huge letdown. My baby was cute, but she wasn't the earth-shattering life experience I wanted. I could have used a proper earth-shattering experience just to jolt me out of depression. Instead, I mentally stood at a tourist trap without a way to get back, and I guess I just camped there, month after month.

'Iolani continued her narrative. "Because I was able to take a step back and really process as much as I could during my maternity leave, when I went back to work, my views on work shifted. My view on my time shifted."

She described the woman I thought I would immediately turn into after becoming a mother. However, while we all understand that there is a "baby lottery," (you may get a baby who is a good sleeper and good eater and is eventually nominated for multiple Nobel Prizes; or you may get a colic-y baby who cries for hours on end . . . and nominated for multiple Nobel Prizes) society doesn't tell us there is also a "mother lottery" (the type of mother YOU would become after giving birth).

Looking back, I chose this once-in-a-lifetime experience. It was underwhelming at first, but there was a child involved now, and I must nourish and cherish my baby as the end-all and be-all of my existence.

Luckily for me, my worldview has shifted enough so I can still cherish my baby but cherish my dreams, too.

Dreams for Your Child

Each day when Jeff picked Rosie up from daycare, she would rush into the kitchen to interrupt my dinner preparation and show me her latest artwork. After receiving proper acknowledgment for each piece of drawing, Rosie would get out her boxes of crayons and colored pencils and a few sheets of my printer paper and return to work.

I would look at her and dream that one day she would be an artist. Perhaps a famous one that has gallery shows in Manhattan. Or a quiet one who spends her time in a log cabin studio in the woods and studies the light dancing over the nearby lake.

I dreamed that she would attend the Rhode Island School of Design. I dreamed that she would backpack through Europe and find her inspiration when crossing the Alps. I dreamed she would meet a grandmaster in Asia who would show her century-old techniques in painting.

When was the last time you dreamed of going on a baking show, making some spectacular showstopper piece that involves a three-foot-high cake? When was the last time you dreamed of opening a yarn shop in a quiet New England town with a floor-to-ceiling wall of rainbow-colored yarn balls? When was the last time you dreamed of writing a book that shows up on the *New York Times* bestseller list and going on a national lecture tour?

It makes perfect sense that once a generation achieves a certain level of success, we look toward the next generation. It's reasonable to nurture them so they can reach a higher level of understanding of the world, make new discoveries, and improve past techniques.

Perhaps, anthropologically speaking, it makes sense for parents to focus their attention on nurturing their children once they join the family. Perhaps in the past, when women were at childbearing age, gave birth, and finished raising their children, they may have been spent and had only enough energy to focus on sustaining their current lifestyle.

But that certainly isn't the case now.

All of us are fortunate enough to live in a society of abundance that allows both our children and ourselves to flourish. So why not allow your imagination to paint the same dreams for yourselves as you do for your kids?

To start, take a few minutes to consider the things that delight you—or once delighted you. Maybe it is the career

It is so easy for us to dream for our children. When was the last time we dreamed for ourselves?

you are currently in where you are energized by the work your organization is doing. Perhaps it is your family and community—your partner, parents, siblings, friends, and neighbors. It could be a hobby you had in the past or something you long to try your hand at. It can also be something you've seen others tackle and accomplish: build a house, travel the world, start a movement . . .

Write them down. All of them. Elaborate on what they are and the path you may take to reach them.

Dreams for Yourself

On Christmas day of 2022, I found a quiet spot in my house with a pen, my planner, and a cup of cocoa. This is a typical time of the year for people to compose their New Year's resolutions. I wanted to make a list for the upcoming year but was stumped.

Rosie was three years old then, and I had barely made it out of my postpartum depression haze. There were words on my paper, but none of them excited me: get a promotion at work, lose ten pounds, do yoga regularly, find my style and create a capsule wardrobe, organize home, learn Japanese, and take a trip to Japan . . .

It was the same list of goals I had for myself year after year, and always for the upcoming year.

I had an enlightening moment—if I write any of those goals down for 2023, the same thing will happen. I will most likely make some progress on some but end up exactly where I am now after 365 days.

It felt like *Groundhog Day*, with the only difference being Rosie growing one year older and I would be living this until she turns eighteen and moves out of the house.

It felt scary and completely unacceptable. *There must be more to my life than raising a child.*

I went into the closet and grabbed all my planners. Every one I had kept since 2016. Each year, in addition to the next year's goals, I also wrote down a list of lifetime goals. Flipping through the books, I saw the same list every year: reach financial freedom, become CFO, travel the world, have a family, write a book, start a nonprofit . . .

I wrote those lifetime goals down for 2023. Why not? It's not like realistic, attainable annual goals would serve me better.

In January 2023, with that fresh-start new year boost, I opened my planner to work on my goals for that year. The most actionable item on the list was to write a book. I thought I would write a children's book. How hard could it be? I've read stacks of them since Rosie was born. And the idea of writing a book to tell Rosie how much I love her and to go the duck to sleep really appealed to me.

I sat down to compose a story. Nothing came. I tried harder. Still no. Absolutely nothing. Zip, nada, zilch . . . A brain full of crickets was composing a symphony in my head. Perhaps writing a book for grownups would be easier.

I thought about what I could possibly say in the form of words that would contribute to this world. The thoughts of my struggle during the first couple of years of motherhood came to mind. The quiet despair, the hours that I spent lying on the floor unable to move, all the research I did to put together tools that would uplift my current condition (and what was turning into my most common floor posture), just to get back to normality . . .

And that, my readers, was the origin story of this book.

Now, I'm starting to dream bigger.

For example, I would like to start a publishing house. It is a romantic notion that really appeals to me.

I would have a small office near my home with an easy commute. The office would have white walls with bright accent colors, some comfortable couches, ergonomic desks and chairs and large monitors, perfect for editing manuscripts.

I would hire a few talented and creative editors and one spunky marketer, and we would all be great at our jobs. I would pay them a good wage with big bonuses, and we would have champagne every time we launched a book.

Together, we will publish smart and entertaining books that spread diverse ideas. Not too many at first, perhaps half a dozen a year, tops . . .

"You have to dream
before your dreams
can come true."
—A. P. J. Abdul Kalam

Pulling the Thread

Dreams and goals often get confused with one another. Both describe a desirable future state, but dreams are bigger and more emotionally charged.

Our society does not encourage us to chase dreams after a certain age. While we encourage children plenty to dream big and be anyone, achieve anything, adults are asked to hold back and do something productive (often for the family or community) with their lives.

Here is the interesting thing—many popular gurus help us achieve our goals by asking us to imagine what those goals lead to, or how the world will open up once we achieve our goals.

The reason is to instill passion into the emotionless SMART (specific/measurable/achievable/realistic/time-bound) goals so we will actually take action. To me, that seems backward and counterproductive since we often end up having logical, reasonable goals on our planner without truly validating whether those are our dreams.

Take "get a promotion" as an example. While it may be the right goal for you after graduation and landing your first job, it may be the completely wrong goal for you as a mother.

Motherhood Is a Long Game

My child is a singer. When she's playing by herself, I can often hear her unabashedly butchering some children's rhyme, filling the air with nonsense lyrics she partially learned from daycare.

I observe Rosie doing plenty of things wrong. She strings L-M-N-O-P together like some unknown word in the English language when she sings the alphabet song. Occasionally, she still struggles to write her own name. Yet, I have no trouble believing she will be able to read *Anna Karenina* someday; the only question is whether she will want to.

Rosie will one day figure out the alphabet, then she will learn to write it. She'll continue to struggle with reading and spelling until they become second nature. One day, she will be reading short paragraphs instead of sentences in a picture book. Once she gets the hang of reading, she may begin to find joy in the act and develop a habit of reading daily.

We take for granted that children will grow from babbling nonsense to speaking and writing fluently, so we should apply this same belief to ourselves.

Many of us look toward motivational speakers to get energized. As inspirational as these public figures are, they never address the issue of achievability—if it is even possible to get to where I want to be. While no one will ever say something is impossible, there may be a voice inside your mind asking, "But is it possible for me?"

This is where being a mother helped me believe.

The world keeps changing, and there are unknown forces at work. I am personally optimistic that my daughter will see better days when she's ready to step into the world. I also believe that any small steps you can take now will show you that, just like the way Rosie's learning her alphabet, you'll gain momentum and grow.

It is all a matter of time. And both you and I can look forward to many days ahead. After all, we plan on watching our kids grow up, graduate, get a job, perhaps meet someone, and fall in love and even have kids of their own. If you planned on being there for your child, you can add a few of your own dreams onto the journey and watch them come true as well.

The lesson here is being a mother makes it easier to see the long game. Your time horizon is not this year or next year, or even the next five years. It is this lifetime, and perhaps followed by your children's lifetime. And that is more than enough to achieve any dream.

We have years ahead to nurture our own dreams amidst the journey of watching our children grow.

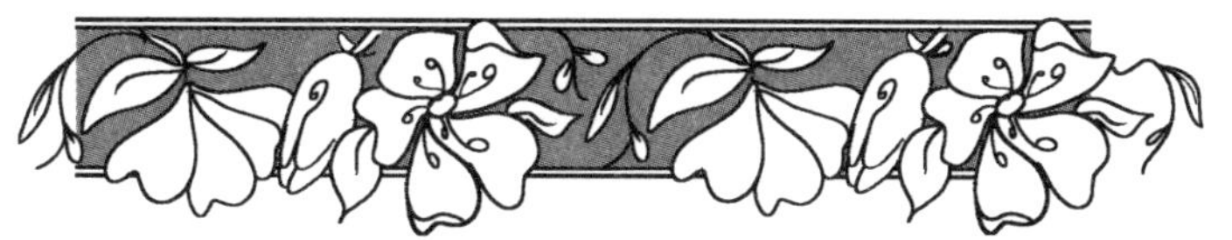

CHAPTER 4

Redefining "Having It All"

"Do you think you can have it all?"

There was a long pause while Sophia considered my question.

I met Sophia in early 2019 when she was a junior studying civil engineering at George Washington University. Sophia was leading a team of student volunteers for Engineers Without Borders (EWB) and was looking for a mentor for their water project for a rural community in Rajasthan, India. I was actively involved in the local professional EWB chapter for several years before finding out that I was pregnant with my daughter. Knowing that I could no longer travel, I sent out a message that I was looking to mentor student chapters while staying put in the DC area.

After a quick introductory call, Sophia and I met at a coffee shop near the GWU campus and really hit it off. I spent the next few months working closely with her team, reviewing their design progress and helping them secure funding for travel. When she and four other students traveled to Rajasthan for site assessment, I connected them with an engineer from New Delhi as their interpreter for the duration of the trip.

Smart, kind, and organized, Sophia has always been a joy to work with. After graduation, Sophia moved to New York City after securing a position at an international engineering firm as a climate adaptation engineer. We were on one of our regular check-in calls when I asked her the question.

"No," Sophia finally replied. Her answer was simple, with a sense of finality. I was shocked at this response—how could someone who is so together, and with her whole life to look forward to, not believe she can have it all?

Sophia and I discussed the finer points of "having it all." This has been our topic of choice for the past couple of conversations—whether a woman can start a family and still make strides professionally.

Even with the most supportive team at work, with a partner, grandparents, or hired help taking over many aspects of child-care, it is incredibly difficult for a mother to put in the same amount of effort as her male or single counterpart at work.

After all, most people spend their careers working for someone else and, since American women don't normally get a lot of help, homelife is work for women as well. That's not "having it all"—that's just working a lot.

One example of this gender discrepancy is when work

demands you "drop everything" without prior notice. As a mother, it is possible to put in the long hours or extensive travels, but it takes a lot of coordination. The type of flexibility required for the most demanding jobs is simply impossible—mothers typically cannot just take an hour to pack their bags and head off to a job site or pick up an evening shift with an hour notice, nor can they consistently put in twelve-hour days or work nightshifts. If those are the requirements to succeed at a certain position, most people would fail, and new mothers are urged to not even try.

On the other hand, being the best mother you can be will require your work life to take a back seat. Even if you have someone doing childcare from nine to five (making it possible for you to have a job at all), there will often be times when you have to drop everything at work to attend to your child. When a child falls sick inconveniently during working hours, they need to be looked at by a healthcare professional.

Moreover, raising a child is thoughtful work. Every child is unique, and it takes a lot of work to understand your child to a point where you can best care for them. While the world understands that it takes training to do any job, sometimes years, many people expect you to become a mother immediately after delivering your firstborn. Most of us are self-taught mothers—this means that even when we're physically at work and not with our children, we're often thinking about the business of being a mom.

One way to look at it is this—caring for a newborn is equivalent to the most demanding job. It's day shift and night shift work, and you're thrown into the mist with neither training nor a manual, with only your ingenuity and whatever resources you have on hand.

Therefore, the premise of "having it all," if it means a devoted mother and thriving at your career, is ludicrous. Especially for any new parent.

Sophia seemed to have come to the same conclusion after we compared our experiences and dove deeper. "You can have everything," Sophia corrected. "You can have a happy life, be a working professional and a mother, but not without sacrificing in some ways or rebalancing."

I agreed.

Then, after pondering that further, I began to disagree.

Are we seriously telling ourselves that being a good mother and a good worker bee is the end all and be all? That we're so bought into this narrative we even agreed to label it as "having it all"? To unpack this complicated phrase and concept, we'll look at the data together and determine if it's worth the effort to "have it all," and how we can tailor this expression to our family dynamics and our personal aspirations.

Women and "Having It All"

We often hear that women can't "have it all."

In 2004, Dr. Sylvia Ann Hewlett published an article in

the *Harvard Business Review* (HBR), titled "Executive Women and the Myth of Having It All."[1]

In her 2001 study, she separated out two groups of women, those who were between the ages of forty-one and fifty-five at the time and those who were twenty-eight to forty. Her criteria for high-performance for these women were an income of $55,000 for the older generation and $65,000 for the younger generation. She also made a category called "ultra-achievers" for those earning more than $100,000.

Hewlett concluded twenty years ago that having a top corporate job and a family was damn near impossible and probably even undesirable. If you truly want to try anyway, Hewlett recommends that women find a spouse, have a child, then choose the right career and company, in that order. Perhaps after giving your dreams a chance during your early years, you may have the life you've intended by the age of forty-five.

Let us step back for a minute to get a better understanding of Hewlett and her point of view. Dr. Sylvia Ann Hewlett is a Cambridge educated economist. She has taught at Cambridge, Columbia, and Princeton universities. The articles she penned were published in the *New York Times*, the *Financial Ties*, and the *Harvard Business Review*. Her book, *Creating a Life: Professional Women and the Quest for Children*, which gives a deeper dive of her HBR article, was endorsed by former US senator and thought leaders of her day. In other words, Hewlett is the archetype of the highly driven career woman, and her advice was meant for women with that same ambition.

Laura Vanderkam is a mother of five kids and the author of over half a dozen books (at the time of this writing, she has nine books published). Vanderkam disagrees with Hewlett's version of our narrative, which is to acquire a husband + children, aligning yourself with a company that values work-life balance, then wish for the best.

"In the discussion of women's life choices, we often focus on the crazy moments, or the difficult moments," wrote Vanderkam. "But these campfire stories built around the dark moments miss the complexity of life."[2]

Vanderkam is saying that the debate of whether women can "have it all" requires more context and nuance than the horror stories provide.

The human mind gravitates toward stories. People tend to tell each other stories as a way to make sense of the world, help us retain information, and pass along learned lessons. Today, our society tells a story of: you can't have it all, so don't even try.

This arguably backward narrative drove Vanderkam to create her Mosaic Project, which she describes in *I Know How She Does It*: "In 2013, I began seeking out time logs from women who, by at least one definition, had it all:

- They earned more than $100,000 per year at the time, and

- They had at least one child (under the age of eighteen) living at home."

Earning six figures while caring for children is a narrow definition of "having it all." But we have to start somewhere.

But is it truly impossible to have both at some point in our lives? Does climbing the corporate ladder really have to consume all of our time and leave no room for home life?

A study quoted in Vanderkam's book, the *Executive Time Use Project*, was run by the London School of Economics and Political Science. One analysis of over one thousand CEOs in six countries saw an average of 52 hours of work per week. The bottom quartile worked 44.2 hours per week, while the top quartile worked 58.5 per week.

Forty-five hours is close to the definition of full-time and may not support the burnt-out narrative. On paper (without context surrounding work conditions or pay), it sounds more like a productive workweek of someone who has their shit together. Perhaps life is not as chaotic at the top of the corporate food chain?

A Narrow Definition of "Having It All"

Ah, the good old days when an annual salary of $55,000 was considered top 10 percent by the Harvard Business Review. The two generations described in Hewlett's study would both be considered boomers. The youngest of her samples would be an elderly Gen X (don't get offended by the description of "elderly"—I am one too).

I want to dive deeper into Vanderkam's study and what it means for modern women. Vanderkam did not state the ages of the Mosaic Project population, but let's assume they are between twenty-five and forty-five.[3] These are your Gen Xers.

Next, let's look at income described in the two studies:[4]

$55,000	in 2001	=	$96,678.44	today
$65,000	in 2001	=	$114,256.34	today
$100,000	in 2001	=	$175,778.98	today
$100,000	in 2013	=	$133,658.59	today

As a baby boomer, you would be described as a high achiever for earning over $96,678.44 and an ultra-achiever if you earn over $175,778.98 per year. For those Gen Xers, the bar for high achievers is raised to earning over $133,658.59 per year.

There are two reasons outlined in Hewlett's HBR article that summarize why she believed high-achieving women don't actually "have it all":

- No husband—these women are picky
- No time—career takes up too much time

When Hewlett says "no time," she means: "29 percent of high achievers and 34 percent of ultra-achievers work more than fifty hours a week."

Hewlett's breakdown of these women's lives went like this: fifty-five-hour workweek plus forty-five minutes for round-trip commute equals thirteen-hour workdays. Plus "extras" for out-of-town trips, client dinners, work functions, etc.

What I find interesting is that both Hewlett and Vanderkam interviewed women who described the consulting-partner career track as not their ideal lifestyle. They currently travel to the client site on Sunday night, put in sixty-plus hours of work, then fly back on Friday to spend the precious weekend with friends and family. When the consultants became partners, their lives were observed to be just as busy and stressful.

"I looked at the senior women in my firm," said a young female interviewee, "and there was no one whose life I wanted.[5]

"Hewett's interviewee, another young woman from a consulting firm, expressed this sentiment: "I know a few hard-driving women who are climbing the ladder at consulting firms, but they are single or divorced and seem pretty isolated. And I know a handful of working mothers who are trying to do their half-time thing or the two-thirds-time thing. They work reduced hours so they can see their kids, but they don't get the good projects, they don't get the bonuses, and they also get whispered about behind their backs. You know, comments like, 'If she's not prepared to work the client's hours, she has no business being in the profession.'"[6]

"How much of this reporting is actually true? And isn't it interesting that many single women hear these kinds of stories and tell themselves that it's safer to stay single than try to reach the same career goals as a parent?

I would like to believe that the professional world we live in is more accepting of diversity—that both our companies and our clients' companies understand that happy, well-rounded people bring more to the table. That is certainly the case from my own experience.

But regardless of my experiences, what mothers need in order to excel is more resources. No matter how accepting those around us are, if we are worn out by our circumstances of balancing work and family, no degree of understanding will help us move the needle forward in our careers.

Furthermore, life is not just about working in the office and working at home. We want to spend time with friends, travel to foreign places, expand our knowledge in any field that captures our interests, put effort into hobbies and crafts, and serve our communities.

I wrote this book to provide more resources (e.g., time, money, energy, and space) to those who are not afraid to dive right into the messiness of life and expect to have it all.

A Balancing Act

For the first year of Rosie's life, I had to keep an eye on her every minute she was awake. In the beginning, I was afraid I was going to break this baby. After months went by and I was sure that she was made of stronger stuff than porcelain, I still had to follow her around to make sure she didn't get hurt.

Productivity experts often tell us not to multitask because the brain is essentially switching between the tasks, as it can only focus on just one. Mothers have to multitask all the time.

Worse yet, I had to set aside all of my passion projects. In my twenties and early thirties, I operated as though every free moment was a waste of life. When I graduated from college and got my first job, I found weekday evenings awfully dull. So I went and got a part-time job as a cook at a restaurant near home. I've also volunteered, mentored, traveled, learned to quilt, learned photography, started and ended a food blog (blogging is truly time consuming), got two advanced degrees (MSE and MBA), got multiple professional certifications (PE,

PMP, and Six Sigma Yellow Belt) . . . the list went on. I never wanted to stop learning, growing, and challenging myself.

And then, everything halted. I had a baby, and she required my constant attention.

I also had five times more laundry, a sink full of dishes, a house scattered with toys, and a very disheveled new look that was threatening to become permanent.

This is not how I want to live my life, I thought. This isn't how anyone wants to live their lives.

It took me a while to realize that I could either continue this lifestyle of catching up (always a step behind on house chores, barely making advances at work, and literally running around my daughter and trying to catch her), or I could change.

In all honesty, after Rosie grew up a bit and I got better with caring for her and myself, things didn't seem that bad. She is an adorable and smart little girl who puts a smile on my face every time I see her. And once she was able to walk and talk (after age one and age two, respectively), I was able to see some light at the end of the tunnel where one day I may be able to get back to some of my old hobbies again.

But do I really want to keep compromising and sacrificing, telling myself that it's going to get better when she grows just a little older? The world is full of amazing people doing exceptional things. Am I really satisfied to never be able to join their ranks, perhaps putting all my hopes and dreams on my daughter for her to achieve instead?

How Motherhood Is Equated to Sacrifice

At some point, you will realize that you may be running out of resources.

There is a "cost" to every lifestyle—the minimal amount of time, money, and energy required to ensure you have a roof over your head, a bed to sleep in, proper nutrition, and the appropriate amount of grooming to be socially presentable, as well as the mental space to create and organize this lifestyle. This is what Maslow might describe as taking care of a person's most basic survival needs.

When you start a family, there is a sharp rise in the resources required of your life. We don't always notice this right away, until our prior way of life starts to slip. Our kitchen gets messier, we wash our hair less often, our bank balances drain lower . . . This usually prompts an examination of your goals, resulting in delaying some goals and letting go of others altogether. The whole process may feel like rebalancing at best or sacrificing at worst. This is referring to the support activities that must take place to get you out of the door and go about your day.

Furthermore, you are putting in less of your ever-dwindling resources into areas unrelated to your child. You no longer work overtime at the office, and that travel fund you were building up is being siphoned off to pay for diapers. The writing on the wall is clear: you are not going to be promoted this year, nor will you be visiting Paris.

Now we can see where the ideas that motherhood is about

sacrificing and rebalancing come in. So let's determine that fine line to avoid the pitfalls of sacrifice and martyrdom.

On the one hand, parents are trying to figure out what it takes to keep their head above water with a new child. On the other hand, their past goals are starving for attention. The story that many mothers tell themselves is that this is the time in their lives where they focus on nurturing their children and growing their family; there will be time for other aspects of their lives sometime later. After all, that's how we get to "have it all," right?

Deep down inside, I hope you know what I'm saying is true. Although the needs of your family may change over time, the steady depletion of your energy will stay the same. Your sacrifice will continue until the kids leave home, either to college or when they find steady employment. And that is a long time from now.

By accepting the idea that you must deny yourself now and defer your own desires, you are reducing your ability to ever achieve your dreams in the future.

How This Book Can Help You

Wherever you are on your journey of motherhood, I want to show you that you are at the beginning of your best and most fulfilling life. It is not fulfilling just because you have a family that brings you unspeakable joy, but because you are the one deciding the future and can clearly see that you will arrive at the destination of your dreams.

To get closer to "having it all," you will have to do two things:

- Dream bigger for yourself, and
- Address any resource deficit—more time, money, energy, and space for yourself

The Lesson

The sudden increase of what it takes to smoothly run a home, now with a baby, is a challenge for every new mother. It is something we can rarely prepare for, as the caring for young children must take place every minute while they are awake. This is the motherhood experience.

As our children grow and we finally get a handle on our new life, it is easy to slip into the mindset of "giving up on yourself" and "sacrificing for the children" simply because we cannot see how to live otherwise.

This is the reason that every mother should dream big for themselves. It jolts us into action, shifts our paradigms, and gives us energy to make that quantum leap in our mindset we need to make the big changes in our lives so we can do more for ourselves while not comprising the care we need to give to our family and home.

In my lighter moments, I would daydream for the favorite people in my life. Sophia, for example, would move abroad and live in Lisbon. I imagine the beautiful, sunny city would really suit her. She would quickly fall in with a group of expats and explore Europe together on holidays. Among her new group of friends, there would be someone she would gravitate toward—a quiet intellectual who appreciates her hard work and wants to walk alongside her as she changes the world.

Together, they would talk about moving back to the States. Maybe to Portland, Oregon, or Austin, Texas, but eventually settle on Denver, Colorado. There, both of them would find work they are passionate about and start a family . . .

And here, I paused. Then what?

Would Sophia join the statistics and become the one in seven women with postpartum depression? Or part of the 43 percent of women who leave the workforce after becoming mothers? While I believe there is great joy in whatever life path we decide to choose and cherish, this may not be in line with "having it all." I wonder if this is what Sophia is also worried about for herself.

I emailed Sophia, wanting to learn more about her hesitation in our prior call. The two of us had a long chat about the timeline of "having it all." I found that although Sophia can see the normal progression of many aspects of life, such as career and personal finance, she is uncertain whether she will be able to fully direct her future when she becomes a mother.

"I think of 'having it all' being all in professionally, and all in as a mother, as well as in one's self-care," Sophia described. "To me, that seems impossible, not that a happy balance can't be achieved . . . but this idea of having it all feels more nuanced to me."

Digging deeper, the nuance Sophia spoke of includes

To truly "have it all," aim higher for yourself and address any resource gap in time, money, energy, and space.

"freedom of expression, energy, mental clarity, and ambition." All of which she associates with being in a younger stage of one's life.

I agree that those are not exactly the words that we conjure up when talking about becoming new mothers. Bringing a child into existence and emerging his new cadence into the mother's life is already a big endeavor.

So, what do I want for myself and other women? I would prefer we reach self-actualization, the peak of Maslow's hierarchy. Or, in other words, reach our full potential. To do so, we have to first understand ourselves and understand what our own potential is.

Having gone through the transition to motherhood, I've personally experienced that those first few years went exactly the opposite of self-actualization. I was depressed, confused, and always exhausted. I was just trying to get by, one minute at a time.

I want to change our definition of "having it all" to be more about ourselves, expect more from that phrase, and keep our minds open to the future.

For those who are contemplating the journey of parenthood, this may be the biggest leap of faith: you will come out on the other side stronger than when you went in.

"Having it all" has a bad rep, and the world continues to tell us it cannot be done. You may be like Sophia—when asked, you may be compelled to say "no" because "having it all" seems like such a big brag. The hope is that with your partner and support system, you'll create your own definitions of enough and balancing career and family that suit you rather than the flawed, outdated expectations of onlookers.

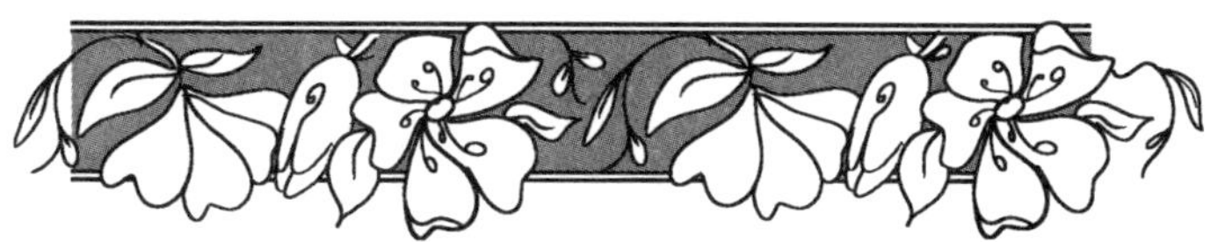

CHAPTER 5

More Time

"You have so much free time!"

This was said to me years ago by my cubemate (yes, this was back in the ancient times when not only did many workers go to the office every single workday, they sometimes shared these working spaces called cubicles with their colleagues).

I was a newbie engineer, and Bruce was my unofficial mentor. The two of us had an unspoken agreement: he got to lecture me on all things work and life, and I got to spontaneously doze off while he talked to me. I found most of his antics rather boring.

On that particular day when Bruce made his remark, I was rushing out the door so I could beat traffic going to a party downtown. I remembered thinking, *What are you talking about? I won't be home until 2:00 a.m. Clearly, I am very busy.*

"You'll see once you have children" was his reply, correctly reading my mind.

Before and After Children

In my childfree days, there were only a few things I had to get right each day: wake up, brush teeth, get dressed, and the universal check of phone-wallet-keys before heading out the door. At work, I was expected to complete a string of manageable yet challenging tasks and wait for someone to check my deliverables before presenting them to the client. In the evenings, I found ways to feed and entertain myself before calling it a night. Rinse and repeat.

Compare that with the roles and responsibilities of a mother, which is described by feminist Adrienne Rich as the "expectation to fill the part of [the] cook, scullery maid, laundress, governess, and nurse" in her book *Of Woman Born*.[1]

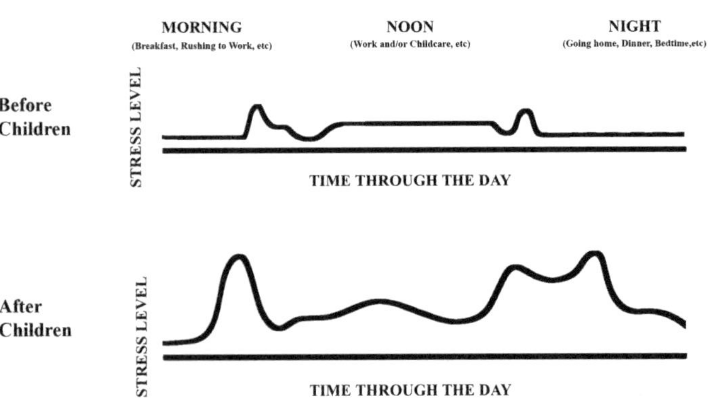

In his book, *The Manager Mom Epidemic*, Dr. Thomas Phelan wrote, "[The] burden for Mom often includes the new household tasks associated with a new baby, such as extra laundry, bottle washing, and shopping."[2] Phelan, a clinical psychologist, helped many families reach a better distribution of household chores. He describes the shock of an increase in mothers' workloads after the first child comes along.

Phelan missed a few things in his description. Parents who like their children also buy them toys and books. For a child to enjoy these gifts, they tend to spread out all of these worldly possessions, which would extend magically to cover every square inch of floor space available in a room. All of these toys need to be picked up should you wish to see the color of your flooring at some point.

Another time-consuming task is making dinner. While researching this book, I read a few dozen childcare books as well as productivity books. Any of the self-help volumes would have anecdotes of mothers describing themselves as "short order cooks." Small children who are still developing their taste buds often dislike the colorful adult food that parents put on the dinner table. In this case, and in order not to starve your offspring, parents prepare a separate children's meal, sometimes making the task of cooking twice as long.

To sum it up, the mother's daily narrative goes something like this: wake up, brush teeth, put on a standard mom's uniform, try to feed and clothe children, and rush everyone out the door for school and office. After the end of the workday, moms are picking up children and perhaps transporting them to various extracurricular activities. Then it is preparing a double dinner, helping children with homework, or entertaining them until bedtime. Lastly, bath, brush, book, bed. Somewhere in there, parents have to fit in the cleaning, laundry, shopping for food, planning (vacation and finance, etc.) and enjoying any self-care activities to keep the body and home running. This was what Bruce meant when he referred to my "free time."

So is it all hopeless? Once the kid arrives, do we no longer have time to do anything else? And what about work and career advancements? How do we even fit that in? Finally, after everyone else gets a share of us, is there time for self-care?

It is not hopeless. Plenty of households run well—everyone gets lots of love and nourishment and the mother can make a difference in the workplace while taking care of her mental and physical health.

Yet, there is still a narrative in our society that women cannot "have it all."

The Atlantic ran an article in its July/August 2012 issue titled "Why Women Still Can't Have It All."[3] The author, Anne-Marie Slaughter, talked about leaving government two years after achieving her dream job: the first woman director of policy planning at the State Department. While sipping champagne at a glamorous evening reception, she was also berating herself for not being there for her fourteen-year-old son through his struggles. This is when Slaughter had an epiphany—she could no longer keep her job and have the homelife she wanted.

Slaughter was in academia before (and after) her State Department position. She taught a full course load at Princeton, regularly contributed to columns on foreign policy, gave dozens of speeches a year, and regularly appeared on TV. That was the backdrop of her life while raising two kids with her husband. It wasn't until her government service position, where she spent two years in Washington, DC, with long weeks and rigid bureaucracy, did she realize that she couldn't do the balancing act in *that* job. She also concluded that it is impossible to "have it all" in certain jobs.

While the article may be written with good intention, it shocks me that we would discourage women (or anyone) from pursuing their dream jobs, however inflexible those jobs may be right now. Our world needs talented individuals to solve a myriad of problems. The existing flexible work environments are a result of the majority of people currently in the workforce. It is my belief that the workplace will change as a response to adding more diversity into the talent pool. Those rigid job structures will only change when enough of us are willing to show up with our talent and diversity to change them to fit the needs of all individuals.

Slaughter, and other women, are trailblazers. They will see that change does come slowly, and their courage in stepping up has started that change.

Do not get discouraged if a job or a career you long for does not currently have paid maternity leave, or demands super long hours, or has insane travel schedules. Go for those positions anyway. The job situation may change when you arrive, or you may receive help in your personal life to make it all work. You will never know how it will all turn out if you get intimidated before you get to the starting line. Moreover, if, like Slaughter, you find yourself in a position that is too rigid to change, you can always leave. When you leave, you will be taking your accomplishments and experience with you. That is what will enrich your life.

After the pandemic, more companies have flexible work policies where there is a combination of remote and office work. Many workers are also actively seeking out more meaningful careers. However, the majority of US workers still do not have that flexibility of choosing remote work.[4] There are industries facing layoffs and families requiring multiple jobs to make ends meet. Knowing these difficulties, it is important to put some planning in place and actively create the work-life balance that is personal to you. I will show you how later in this chapter.

"The human brain is structured for loss aversion," said Laura Vanderkam in her book *I Know How She Does It*, "and so negative moments stand out more starkly than positive moments, particularly if they fit a popular thesis.[5]

This means that Slaughter and others who have experienced burnout and the regret of not being fully present to their families may emphasize the most hurtful moments of their experiences rather than the smaller joyful ones. Even more important is that people who are doing just fine are not pressing *The Atlantic* to have their most triumphant moments published. Success stories are not news; they're just common everyday experiences.

Let's not look at other people's horror stories and tell ourselves, "I don't want that." I've met many young professionals who shy away from career advancement, presupposing that the next rung of the corporate ladder will lead to an excess of work and not enough time for a future family. They would look at their company's leadership and, unintentionally, create a backstory for each person. This partner must not ever see their children, or that manager probably doesn't spend enough time with their spouse.

The truth is that people often create a work persona where they may appear to be overworked and under stress, or in some other way that outwardly shows that they are working hard for the company. Unless you hang around that partner or manager, you won't know whether they have an undesirable life or not.

Chances are, however, that your senior management team would not approve of you tagging along with them once they're off work. Therefore, I urge you to get to that level of career success, with partner and children first.

And if you still find yourself socializing with President and Mrs. Obama at an evening reception at the Natural History Museum (like Slaughter was when she had her epiphany moment), then take the steps to balance out your life. Perhaps then, you will be able to keep the good, negate the bad, and have it all. Of course, having it all is easier said than done. Let's dive deeper into what this can look like realistically.

New Perspective on Your Time

We looked at a lot of the pieces of this puzzle (career, childcare, homecare, and self-care) and it's time to put everything together. To start, let's first examine your career time horizon and work out where are the best places to carve out time to start and nourish a family.

This does not mean we are putting a company's needs before our own. Your occupation is your dedicated craft—something you will be developing throughout your entire life and will act as your channel through which you contribute to our world and society.

Plan and Build Your Time

Regardless of who you talk to, women who have succeeded in the career and family balancing act will tell you it was not by chance. There was a lot of intention that went into planning—not just on a daily or weekly level but spanning multiple years. Understanding this type of "big picture" planning will help direct your efforts into the area of life that needs most tending.

For example, stabilize your career before you start a family, or build a network of supporters before getting back into the workforce. Keep in mind that even if you do this, not everything will be in your control.

But you may also be surprised at how little time it takes to influence decision-makers and alter your trajectory. Add a dash of luck, and you will find a lifestyle that is more palatable than the burnt-out working mother narrative.

You want to first examine your chosen field of work and its advancement time horizon. This is less industry-dependent and more based on who is paying your salary. Are you part of a large corporation? A smaller company? Or starting your own enterprise? Perhaps freelancing with a portfolio of projects?

Find out where you can expect to go in five, ten, and fifteen years if you stay at the same company and you are performing well each year. To advance within your career is not just about money. You should also gain personal fulfillment as well as contribute to the society you live in.

Let's go through an example of how to map out this work-life balance using the standard advancement for a consulting firm.

With an undergraduate degree, you can get hired as an analyst. This position typically takes three to four years of solid exceptional performance to become promoted to consultant, with an intermediate step as senior analyst.

Analyst (18 Months) → Senior Analyst (2 Years) → Consultant

As a consultant, it should take you between three and five years to become a manager. Alternatively, going back to school to get an advanced degree can help solidify your role and become a subject matter expert in your field.

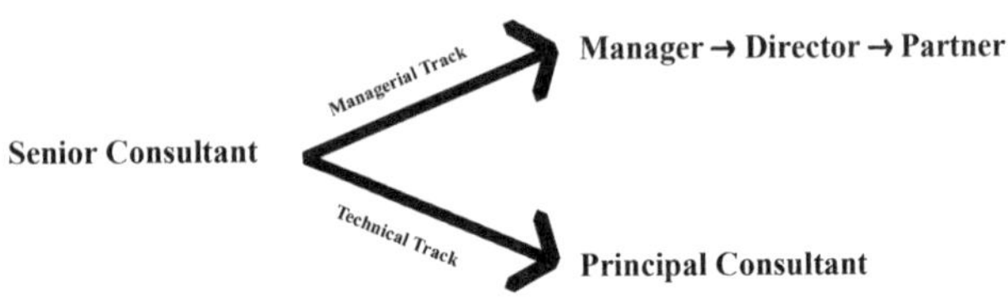

Managerial track would allow you to continue to rise within the company, eventually becoming a partner of the firm. This track is also an outward facing role: you'll be communicating with clients, eventually bringing in projects by convincing clients to give you more work.

The technical track allows you to stay within your field and work toward deepening your knowledge. You may need an advanced degree, published papers, and to network with others in the same field to be up-to-date on the latest innovations.

Regardless of which track you choose, you can expect a promotion every three to five years at the beginning of your career. Later, the waiting time will be longer (five to seven years) as you tackle the higher rungs of the ladder.

Take this journey and overlap it with your age. Say you graduated from college at twenty-two and took a year off to explore the world. When you return, you begin working at a large firm in its entry-level position.

Write out your age, year by year, and use the guide that you should be expecting a promotion every three to five years. If you are in one of the Big Four consulting firms, you can use the career path that I wrote out above. Plan on having one to two years of stagnation every now and again (perhaps between going from a consultant to a senior consultant or from senior consultant to manager). The constant grind of getting to the next rung of the career ladder can be tiresome, not to mention absolutely boring in your social life.

Adding slack to your career trajectory can give you the peace of mind that you are exactly where you're supposed to be, even if another promotion is not in the cards for that year or the next.

YEAR	YOUR AGE	TITLE & TIME IN POSITION
2024	*23*	*Analyst, Now*
2025	*24*	*Analyst, 1 year*
2026	*25*	*Senior Analyst (promotion year)*
2027	*26*	*Senior Analyst, 1 year*
2028	*27*	*Consultant (promotion year)*
2029	*28*	*Consultant, 1 year*
2030	*29*	*Senior Consultant (promotion year)*
2031	*30*	*Senior Consultant, 1 year*
2032	*31*	*Senior Consultant, 2 years*
2033	*32*	*Senior Consultant, 3 years*
2034	*33*	*Senior Conultant, 4 years*
2035	*34*	*Manager (promotion year)*
2036	*35*	*Manager, 1 year*
2037	*36*	*Manager, 2 years*
2038	*37*	*Manager, 3 years*
2039	*38*	*Manager, 4 years*

Getting to Cruising Altitude

So, where does a family fit into this picture? Where do you squeeze in the time to conceive, give birth, and change diapers?

One way is to take time off. Women start their careers, then take a few years off to focus on caring for their kids while they're young. After the children get to school age and are no longer at home, mothers typically go back and join the workforce.

This is a good plan. It does not involve juggling responsibilities and will allow you to stay focused on a single aspect of your life at a time. The downside is that your career usually gets a "restart" when you return, even if you are returning to the same position with the same company. That is to say, if you've worked a couple of years at one position, you are likely to repeat those years while waiting for your promotion.

An alternative is to plan on starting a family while working full time, with a short break for maternity leave. The trick to this plan is timing.

"When you're trying to build a career, a reputation, or your personal brand, you really need to focus on yourself," said Jay Prescott, Director of Global SOC Operations at Rapid7, a cybersecurity company. Jay's crew is stationed all over the world, and he spends much of his time hiring, training, and mentoring those at various stages of their careers.

I asked Jay what he would recommend for those with a long career runway and are considering when to start a family.

"You don't want to be too distracted when you're continuing education or finding what makes you happy. You want to spend the time getting really good at what you do. Once you get to a point where your day-to-day is stable, that is a good time to expand and perhaps bring a child into the world."

"The very early years [of motherhood] are going to slow your career down," said Kristin Homsi, a mother of two and manager of supply chain at Bechtel Corporation, when I interviewed her. "Plan for that and be okay with that." Homsi advised to be in a position where you don't have to put your foot 100 percent on the gas pedal for two to three years, then evaluate your career trajectory to make sure you're aligned for the next role. "The preschool years are the hardest, but you will go forward again."

The good news is that this slowdown only applies to your first child. While your second and third child will take up more of your energy and effort, you would have significantly more experience as a mother.

"Janet," Homsi laughed, "by the time you have kid three, you don't even realize that you had an extra kid, you know?"

In other words, you want to get to a cruising altitude with your work before considering expanding your personal life.

Earlier in this chapter, we mapped out a tentative career plan. Looking at your version of the plan, you want to be about nine months to a year into a new job or position before adding more to your plate. This period is to ensure you have time to connect with your colleagues, learn the ropes, and will be able to contribute at the work front without expending your full energy.

If you are with a new company, it is also extremely important to make sure you are there long enough for any maternity benefits to kick in. Make sure you inquire with your HR department.

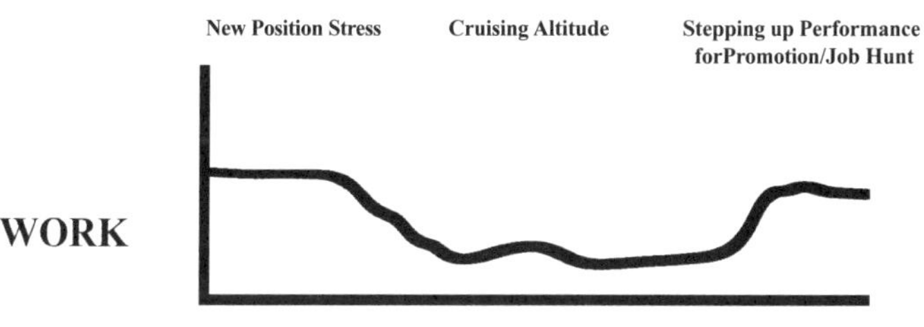

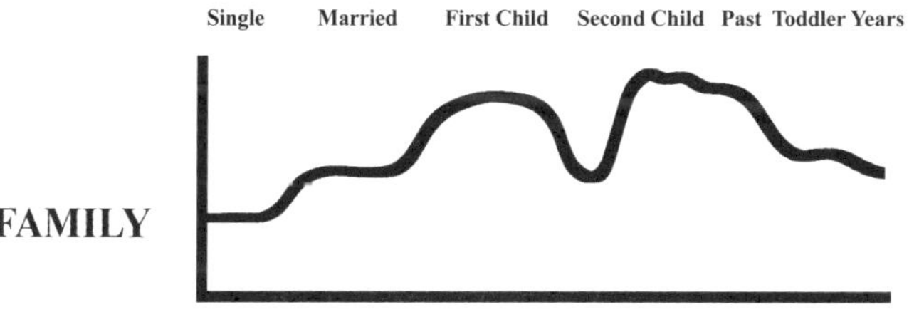

The first two to three years of motherhood are the most intense. Your child will initially require around-the-clock feeding, then a lot of time to bond as well as your care and attention to grow. You will also be learning how to get more efficient operating as a family (for example, getting out the door in less than thirty minutes). All of this means that much of your attention will be focused on your family during those years. Even for those of us who are great at compartmentalizing, there will be days where it will be difficult to operate 100 percent at work.

Having gone through the exercise of planning out your career, this should give you assurance that you're not getting derailed—just temporarily cruising but still on track. However, if you cannot miss a beat at work, or if you're the type to bring her laptop to the hospital and start answering emails just hours after your baby is born, then make sure you set up ample help on the home front.

Skill Tip: Make sure others can do your work and produce the same results.

A skill that will always come in handy is to teach others around you to produce the same result. This doesn't mean delegating, which involves getting someone to actually do certain tasks. We're talking about making sure others can do your work if need be. Many workplaces have a standard operating procedure (SOP) for routine tasks. At home, adults/ parents communicate with each other to ensure everyone is on the same page. The conversation should describe:

- Triggering event
- Your procedure
- Expected result
- An invitation to improve and the importance of the task

For example: "Hey, I just want to share with you my thoughts on cleaning the kitchen. I usually like to do this every night, a few hours past dinner when everyone has time to decompress (triggering event). What I like to do first is clear the table and counter by gathering all the dishes, toss the linens into the laundry basket, then wipe down everything with Clorox wipes. Then I load the dishwasher, scrub the sink, and do a quick sweep of the floors (your procedure).

This way, no food is left out and all the surfaces are cleaned (expected result). You don't have to do it the same way. I just want to let you know that I feel happy and calm when this is done every day, as it signals the end of daily chores for me and keeps the bugs away (why this is important to you)."

In addition to having help with childcare and your own recovery after birth, it would be good to arrange for someone to help clean the house and a way to get food on the table every night.

All of this said, it's important to keep in mind that a career is long. There are years ahead for you to work on your craft and to get to where you'd be proud of when you're at the end of the road. Do not let yourself or anyone else (your child included) distract you from moving forward. See setbacks as temporary breaks or detours, ones that will make the final picture of life more detailed and more rewarding.

Smaller, Daily Details about Work Hours

In the prior section, we looked at work-life balance on the larger time scale. Based on your career trajectory, we considered times when you can scale back at the office for those early years of family life.

In this section, we're looking at the day-to-day when you have to balance your hours spent at work versus those spent at home.

When we assume others are successful at their jobs, we imagine that they work all the time. Maybe they travel to check out vendor sights in person or to face-to-face meetings with the customers. Maybe they're logging eighty-hour workweeks and are rarely at home.

The latest statistics from the United States Bureau of Labor Statistics show that we work just over thirty-two hours per week.[6]

According to historical charts from the St. Louis Fed, the average workweek of an employed worker fell from 42.4 hours per week in 1950 to 39.1 hours per week in 1970. About ten years ago, the US Bureau of Labor Statistics reported a workweek of 34.5 hours. After a decade and a pandemic, we're now down to around 32.3 hours per week.

Looking at the numbers, our society as a whole is not overworked. So where are the higher working hours perceptions coming from?

An earlier study of professional time logs by sociologists John Robinson and Geoffrey Godbey notes that people overclaim higher hours when asked to give a number by the week.[7] When you ask individuals to keep a daily diary, their day-to-day work hours are systematically lower. Robinson and Godbey found that those who are claiming 50 to 45 hours a week were consistently overestimating by nine hours. Those who are claiming between 55- to 59-hour workweeks were off by ten hours, and those who estimated 60 to 64 hours were off by fourteen. If you go higher, those who work 65 to 74 are off by fifteen, and those who claim to work 75+ are off by twenty-five hours.

In a way, Robinson and Godbey's reporting is intuitive. Each of us has a limit of how many hours we can sustainably put in for our job each week. The more hours beyond the average thirty-five hours, the more we want to be acknowledged for those extra efforts. Hence the increase of exaggerated working hours.

When Laura Vanderkam was collecting data for her Mosaic

Project, she would give talks at companies and request participants to keep a time log for one week prior to the event. Using this method, she was able to review time logs of the same week by different people working for the same organization.

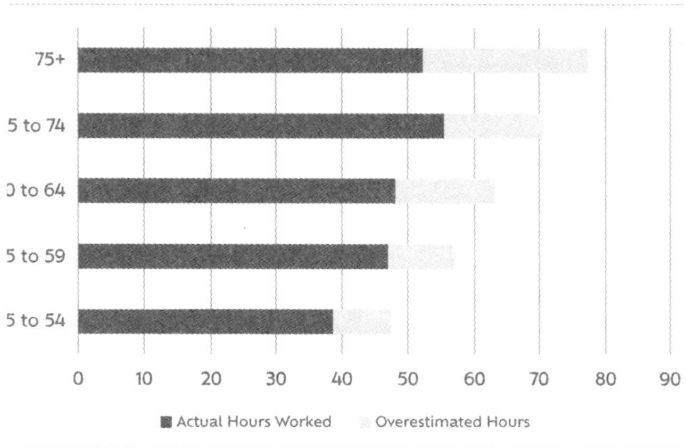

Vanderkam found vast differences between some colleagues' time logs. Often, she would see different workers, both full-time, having as much as a ten-hour gap in any given week. "No doubt that ten-hour gap corresponds to different career trajectories," explained Vanderkam, also from her book *I Know How She Does It*, "but clearly 'full-time' encompasses a host of lifestyle options.[8]

Today, many full-time salaried employees have some sort of flexibility at work. A Deloitte report in 2022 stated that 68 percent of the employees surveyed have a hybrid work

Good enough is perfect—know when to let go, accept the imperfection, and move forward to tackle greater challenges.

model.[9] A 2022 McKinsey article also optimistically claims that 90 percent of the employers would like to move to that model where people may work from home some of the time.[10]

Even if your job does not have a formal policy of part-time work from home, most managers allow for flexibility where parents can pick up their kids from school or schedule doctor's appointments during the normal working hours.

If that is the case for you, then you may really benefit from doing a week-long time log of all of your activities in your waking hours. The purpose is to track the total number of hours you've worked without shortchanging yourself. Many of us put in some time outside of the core working hours—in early mornings, evenings, or on weekends. When you can see the complete picture of your efforts, you may see that you spend more than forty hours on the job.

Say that you find that you work close to fifty hours per week and consciously decide to put in ten hours less work in a particular week. That equates to either two hours per workday doing something else or taking an entire day off. This is a significant enough time when dedicated to another activity to really make an impact on other aspects of your life. On the other hand, we often waste that time when we are logged in at work. A few more extra coffee breaks, some leisurely lunches, or browsing the Internet, the same amount of time may be squandered, leaving us to produce the same quality of work products.

The Pareto principle states that roughly 80 percent of your

results come from 20 percent of your effort. The idea of "good enough is perfect" is knowing the importance of letting go and accepting an imperfect result to let go of this small aspect of your life and move onto something else bigger.

Combining the two concepts produces a powerful time-saver. The 80-20 principle may also explain that ten-hour gap.

Freeing Up Your Time When Working Freelance or Non-Salaried

For those who are not full-time salaried workers, people who work freelance or have multiple jobs, shaving off working hours may seem like a nonstarter idea to you.

I readily agree that it is far more difficult to be managing multiple clients and bosses, each with a unique demand. From my experience, if you are reporting to more than one manager, chances are your "full-time" is more than forty hours.

During the years where I worked as an engineer, there were many times when I had to transition from one project to another. These were tricky situations where the project I was leaving wanted me to stay longer and the project I was entering wanted me to start earlier. We would all compromise by splitting my time in some way where I could work both jobs at once. Say, fifty-fifty fair split down the middle. The problem with these arrangements was that I always ended up working close to full time on both projects, ending with close to eighty-hour workweeks and killing myself without any benefits.

I recommend the following strategies for those who are working freelance, part-time, or with multiple jobs.

Part-Timers

Part-time implies that your employer does not get the whole of your working hours and you get some of the weekdays for yourself. In exchange, you forgo part of your salary. Over the years, I've only seen this work on occasion. The trick is to become very good at setting boundaries—these women do not stay late, and they can put their work down without a second thought.

The drawback to this arrangement is that it is difficult to move your career forward.

When you work part-time, it may be hard for your employer to justify spending additional resources to train you. You may be brought on board to supplement the existing full-time workforce, who would be first in line for promotions, bonuses, and training.

Companies are now looking into flexible work schedules as a way to attract and retain talent. This includes remote work (where you work from home) and flex schedule (where you choose your work hours). If you are currently at a part-time arrangement by choice, it may be beneficial to ask if it is possible to work full-time in the future and what that arrangement may be like. From there, you can use the suggestions in this chapter to carve out the time you need or use the additional income to hire help.

Freelance and Multiple Jobs

"Four years ago, an economist changed my life forever," wrote Tim Ferriss in his book *The 4-Hour Workweek*. "I had been slaving away with fifteen-hour days seven days per week, feeling completely overwhelmed and generally helpless."[11]

The economist Ferriss was referring to was Vilfredo Pareto. The same Pareto mentioned earlier with the 80-20 principle. Specifically, the Pareto principle states that around 80 percent of the consequences come from 20 percent of the causes. In Ferriss's case, he looked for the 20 percent of sources that were causing 80 percent of his headaches, along with the 20 percent of sources that contributed to 80 percent of the desired outcome.

The result for Ferriss was this: "I stopped contacting 95% of my customers and fired 2%, leaving me with the top 3% of producers to profile and duplicate. Out of more than 120 wholesale customers, a mere 5 were bringing in 95% of the revenue. I was spending 98% of my time chasing the remainder . . . because I felt as though I should be doing something from 9-5."

While I find the book title misleading, and many parts of the book bro-ishly cringey, I do agree with Ferriss that it may be helpful to examine all of your income sources from time to time.

Make a list of your clients and jobs. For each, list how much you make per hour, for how many hours per week on average, and the ease of the job or how much you enjoy the work. From that list, consider both the clients who are at the top and at the bottom.

When looking at the top half of the list, ask yourself: can you offer more value and raise your rates? If you enjoy working for a client, chances are the feeling is mutual. Consider setting up a meeting to discuss what other work the client has and the potential to be more involved. If the answer is none, then perhaps ask if your client knows others who may need your services.

I received this note from my illustrator. We'd been working on a children's book and initially agreed on thirty dollars per page:

> *"Dear, I do not want to make you feel uncomfortable or disturbed by my request, but can we make the page for $40? Because I had previously worked on children's stories that were less complex and simple and did not contain many people like these, I felt while working that it took me a lot more time and effort than before. Do you understand me? But if you don't like that, it's okay. We can continue the price we agreed on first because I agreed with you on that from the beginning and I don't want to lose you as a client. I mean, as you like, I just wanted to tell you that, if it's possible, it will be better for me, but I will continue to work."*

I happily agreed to her request.

Now look at the bottom half of the list. How can you

make the most of these clients? Sometimes, we do need all the work we have to make ends meet. If you are in a place where you're comfortable taking a chance, then consider the following options:

- For the work you enjoy but pays little—ask for more money
- For the work you do not enjoy and pays little—ask for a lot more money

Instead of taking Ferriss's approach and "breaking up" with 80 percent of your income-generating work, I would increase your rate instead—drastically, if it is work you hate. Chances are, they will just say no and then you can consider quitting.

Our time is precious. Find ways to free up small amounts of time that can later be consolidated into longer stretches. Later in this book, I will show you how to rearrange your obligations so you can claim the best hours in the day for yourself.

Time with Your Children

When Vanderkam was researching for her book *168 Hours: You Have More Time Than You Think*, a homeschooling mom said she would like to figure out how to spend more time with her kids. "When I say I want more time with the boys, I am wanting more time where they have my undivided attention. I guess because I stay at home and homeschool, we are technically together 24/7 but seldom do they get all of me.[12]

The timeless conundrum of working mothers seems to be thinking about work when we're at home and thinking about home when we're at work.

If we scrutinize every minute of our time, a lot of it is actually spent with our families. Every morning before work/school, every evening before going to bed, and all day on weekends, minus time spent running errands and self-care time. But when we talk about spending more time with our children, what we want is "quality" time, or time spent with "undivided attention" to our children.

This is much harder than just carving out more time in our calendars to be with our kids. Because little kids are adorable and oh so booooring. As a toddler, Rosie did not contribute to any insightful conversations, she often criticized me for playing her games wrong, and we didn't share similar TV interests. Moreover, a great deal of time spent with younger children involves teaching—how to use the potty, how to brush teeth, how to put on shoes—every skill we had long stopped thinking about now needs to be examined, slowly, and repeatedly.

Additionally, it is hard to plan solid bonding moments or schedule when your child will share their amusing antics. It takes a lot of time to get to a state where everyone is calm, content, and good things are happening. Then, in a blink of an eye, that moment is gone because now we have to get to school, or eat dinner, or take a bath . . .

There are couples who divide up childcare tasks (e.g., taking care of breakfast and shuttling kids to school every other day, or one watches the kids before dinner and the other after dinner). Jeff and I have decided to co-parent as often as possible to create more quality time with Rosie.

Except for picking up and dropping off Rosie at daycare, Jeff and I try to be with her together at all times. Since both of us are present, I can find pockets of time to check my phone or to walk away altogether if I feel overwhelmed. The flip side also applies. I can jump right in and engage with Rosie when there is a specifically delightful moment happening, or when I hear Jeff's tune is starting to get a bit weary.

Housework

When organization guru Marie Kondo had her third kid, she gave up the notion to keep her house tidied at all times. "My home is messy," Kondo said in an interview to *The Washington Post*, "but the way I am spending my time is the right way for me at this time at this stage of my life.[13]

It turned out all we had to do to achieve a professional

level of tidiness in our home was to wait for the standard to drop.

Tongue in cheek aside, this should be the permission for anyone who's still trying to keep an Insta-worthy order at home. After trying this for a few years, I think all of us come to the conclusion that a stray sock here and there never killed anyone.

Then again, the heart wants what the heart wants. When it comes to keeping a well-run and tidy home, many of us are still willing to devote significant time to the endeavor. In her Mosaic Project, Vanderkam found that the women devoted as many as twenty-five hours per week on household chores (the lowest was two hours per week while the average was around ten).[14]

The latest American Time Use Survey showed that in 2022, on days they did household activities, women spent an average of 2.7 hours while men spent just 2.2 hours. On an average day, 47 percent of women reported performing housework, while just 22 percent of men reported the same.[15]

Similar to successful women at work, there are women who spend an extra ten hours per week on household chores. While it takes some time to run a household (keep everyone fed, disease-free, and decently clothed), give yourself some slack when trying to create the picture-perfect family in order to get some of your time back.

Working with Your Partner

"Wait, you're telling me that you're *never* going to change diapers?" Jeff asked incredulously, horror showing on his face as the realization dawned that I wasn't joking.

I had just given birth. A nurse was demonstrating how to swaddle and change a newborn's diaper to my husband and me, and I was choosing this time to boycott motherhood.

The third trimester hadn't been kind to me. I could never get comfortable in any position, I had to get up to pee five times each night, and on top of all of that, my darling girl was lodged in a way that she kicked my belly in the exact same spot each time she hiccupped . . . and it felt like she was always hiccupping. When my water finally broke, Jeff rushed me to the hospital only for us to wait half a day until I was fully dilated. I was starving when a kind hospital staff brought me a small cup of lemon ice. My favorite. I was on my second bite when the doctor walked in and took the lemon ice away, saying that it was time to push.

When the delivery ordeal was finally over, I was in no mood to cooperate with anyone. So, I told my poor husband that I was never going to change diapers and he had better pay close attention to the demonstrating nurse.

I did eventually come back to reality and ended my motherhood boycott, but because of that initial incident, Jeff became quite good at swaddling and diaper changing and always took the lead on those tasks from then on. He also realized that, aside from breastfeeding, I had no natural lead on childcare. With some learning and practicing, he could do just about anything that was traditionally assigned to mothers.

Societal norms and motherly instinct tell us that there are many care tasks that belong to mothers. We must care for our children, our husband, our home, and if there is time, ourselves. Two things need to happen to break this—you need to step back and your partner needs to step forward. Here's how.

For the Partner

Open your mind and consider all the possibilities of what care tasks you would like to do. Have you always wanted to try baking a cake or cooking a certain dish you loved growing up? Carve out some time in the kitchen to level up your skills, with the goal of taking over dinner preparation. Browse the cleaning aisle at your grocery store and pick out tools and supplies you like, then dedicate a weekend to try out those cleaners in the bathrooms and kitchen.

Childcare is just as foreign and difficult for new mothers as they are to you right now, and you can become as skilled as any soccer mom with determination and some practice.

How I Do It

Here is a typical weekday for us.

Five a.m. to six a.m.—Either my child or my cat climbs up onto my bed to wake me up. Both cat and child know that I am the one who doles out breakfast this early in the day, so Jeff gets to sleep in more on weekdays.

The procession of mom, child, and cat makes it downstairs, and everyone gets nourishment. Rosie and I usually have yogurt or a banana, and the kitty has kibbles. Rosie likes to eat breakfast in front of the TV, so I get this period of time to write or journal.

Eight a.m.—Jeff wakes up and takes over childcare. This mostly involves coaxing Rosie away from her morning activities into proper school clothes. Jeff drops off Rosie at daycare, unless he is working from the office that day. In which case, I would do the drop-off and send Jeff to the metro station.

Nine a.m.—I start work. I work full-time remote, supporting colleagues around the world. In the morning I normally first check in with the team in New Delhi before they sign off for the day. I would then move onto reading my emails, prioritizing the ones sent from London in case they needed something from me that day.

Mid-morning—Throughout the morning, I tackle housework in small bits. This usually consists of making our beds, making Rosie's bed, picking up clothes and toys from the floor, unloading the dishwasher, and starting a load of laundry. For example, after sending an email, I would go upstairs to make one of the beds. This gets me walking around the house instead of sitting static for hours.

Afternoon—More work. By this point, all my US colleagues are online. We message on Teams and do voice calls. I also schedule blocks of time where it looks like I'm in a meeting, but I'm actually just focusing on getting a single work task completed.

Five p.m.—I stop work. Jeff picks up our daughter from daycare. I cook three times a week—the rest of the days are for leftovers or takeout. At this time, Jeff is again the primary caregiver. They spend the time before dinner drawing chalk outside or watching TV if it is raining.

Evening—This is the unstructured part of our day. Occasionally, we would go to the playground with Rosie or walk to get ice cream. More often, she would play at home by herself while Jeff and I do chores or catch up on some remaining work tasks.

Seven p.m.—This is my favorite time of the day when I start to usher my daughter up to her room. I bring out the large pile of children's books from the library, and we read together. Our current favorite is called *Spike and Cubby's Ice Cream Island Adventure*. When I get to the part of the book where the island comes into view, both my daughter and I yell, "ICE CREAM ISLAND!" Even though I am the primary caregiver at this time, my husband likes to be in the room. He sits quietly on the papasan, listening in on what his girls are doing. Occasionally he helps if I have trouble getting our daughter changed into her pj's.

Eight-thirty p.m.—Child in bed. Alone time. Truthfully, I'm not sure what my dear husband is doing at this time on most days. Today, he wanders into the kitchen to put food away and the dishes in the dishwasher, then wanders somewhere else. If the kitchen isn't clean by my standards and I have some extra energy, I put on a podcast and a pair of heavy-duty cleaning gloves to tackle the grime that only I can see. If I'm tired, I play video games instead.

Nine forty-five p.m.—This is my second favorite time of the day. Jeff and I go back to our room and chat about our day. We like to rehash any favorite moment each of us have had with our daughter. Then we read books or watch TV, shower, then go to bed.

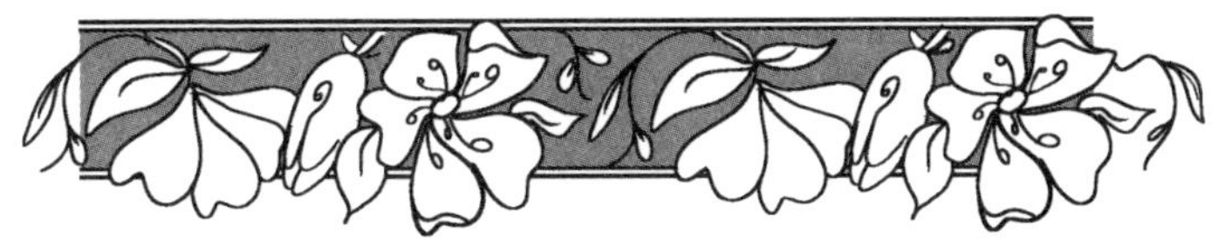

CHAPTER 6

More Money—Part 1

How much does it cost to raise a child? In its latest report, the USDA estimated that it will cost parents $233,610 to raise a child born in 2015.[1] By the time of this writing (in 2023), inflation would have increased this number to a whopping $303,267.[2] This cost is from the birth of a child until they turn seventeen years of age. If spread evenly throughout this timeline, parents would average just under $18,000 per year to raise a child.

What if I tell you that instead of $18,000 a year, you can spend as little as $3,000 in your first year (or just over $250 a month)? Interested? Then read on.

The way USDA puts together this number is first by breaking down childcare costs into seven categories: housing, food, transportation, clothing, health care, childcare and education, and miscellaneous. Over thirty thousand households were surveyed (seven thousand were single-parent families) to see how much of their annual household expenses were child specific.

As I studied the report, I found it interesting that there seem to be these little "jump" in expenses. For households earning less than $59,200, their expenses were between $9,330 to $9,980. That's almost half of the average cost. As the parents' income increases to over $59,200 and under $107,400, the annual expense range jumps to $12,350 to $13,900. This "jump" occurs again for households earning over $107,400. Their annual child-specific expenses were between $19,380 to $23,380.

Since babies are more or less the same since birth, it appears that a certain income level triggers something that lets the parents spend more on their children. You'd spend almost 40 percent more on your child once your income gets past the $60,000 threshold. Similarly with the $107,400 threshold. That group spends 63 percent more than those earning between $60,000 to $107,400, and 122 percent more than households earning below $60,000.

It is natural to spend a little more when you earn more. We want to use our hard-earned dollars to elevate our standard of living and bring more beauty and joy into our lives. Some of that elevation would naturally go into child-specific expenses. However, we must pause to consider the effect of these spendings. A child does not feel as keenly the gain of certain expenses as we do.

Just for fun, let's make a few outlandish assumptions for the spending decisions of a new mom. Say this new mom decided to spend the minimal amount possible on her newborn, with the more expensive items purchased second-hand or donated. This mom will also not make any upgrades to the house or car at this time.

With these assumptions, we can re-estimate her first year of child-specific expenses:

Housing: $500 total

Since she is not moving to a larger home due to an increase in family size, the child-specific cost for this category consists of furnishing (a crib, child gates, etc.) and a minimal increase in utility costs.

Food: $100 initially, $50 per month for half a year

We are assuming that she breastfeeds for most of the first year and starts introducing solids to her baby after six months (as recommended by the American Academy of Pediatrics and CDC).[3] Her child-specific food expenses can be estimated to be around $50 per month for yogurt, oatmeal, applesauce, and avocados. There may be some initial costs for bottles.

Transportation: $150 for car seat, then $5 per month

We are also assuming she will be using her existing car with a new added car seat, which she can get for less than $150. We're adding $5 per month for gas for the child-specific trips she will be taking (to the doctors, to see family, to playgrounds, etc.)

Clothing: $100 total

Believe it or not, Rosie spent her first few months wearing no clothes. Jeff and I were too scared to tuck her tiny arms and legs into onesies, so we mostly wrapped her using the swaddle clothes we got from the hospital. If you belong to an organization (such as a church or a Buy Nothing group), you can get a lot of secondhand baby clothes for free. There are also resale or consignment stores and events (such as Just Between Friends) where you can get baby clothes for a very reasonable price.

Health Care: $0

Another bold assumption is that you have good healthcare coverage, and you have a healthy baby. You will have a few doctor's visits to the pediatrics (cost of getting to the office and back are covered under transportation).

Childcare: $0

This is the biggest assumption here—you or a family member is performing childcare full time. More on this later.

Education: $0

A child's learning during their first year is almost entirely physical (such as crawling, walking, focusing vision, reaching, etc.).[4] As a parent, you are more than enough to teach everything here.

Miscellaneous: $100

The USDA's report defines this category as "personal care items (haircuts, toothbrushes, etc.), entertainment (portable media players, sports equipment, dance lessons, computer games, etc.), and reading materials (non-school books, magazines, etc.).[5] Same as the clothing category, many items within miscellaneous can also be purchased at a low cost.

This comes to $1,610. Far lower than the reported amount.

Is this realistic? Actually, yes. In the budget above, I opted for brand new items that were related to safety (car seat and crib). Even those can be purchased secondhand, after careful inspection to make sure everything is to code and with no damage.

What we need to come to terms with is that anything other than bare essentials are not for the baby; it's for you. A beautiful nursery with an heirloom quality crib, designer bedding, attached with adorable crib mobile, next to a swivel nursing glider chair, a vintage dresser filled with new baby clothes of all ages and for all occasions, contained within newly painted walls with your baby's name spelled out in wall art, custom designed from your favorite Etsy store . . . all of that would be for you. While your child does need to sleep in and wear something, anything above the basics would not be noticed. And this is where most of the cost saving lies.

The Grandmother Hypothesis

The one cost that is extremely difficult to save on is childcare. Our society used to have a solution for this.

Anthropologists developed the "grandmother hypothesis" to explain how grandmothers play a significant role in raising children.[6]

Our species produces a child roughly once every three years. Researchers estimated that a woman has the ability to forage in the wilderness for only enough calories to sustain herself, about 2,000 calories per day.[7] Anthropologists suspected the additional calories required for a mother to feed herself and her young are provided by other family members, often grandparents.[8]

This hypothesis suggests that grandparents play a

"Enough is not too little."
—Morgan Housel, author of
The Psychology of Money

significant role in the evolution of humans. Multiple generations contribute to the care and upbringing of children to increase the chances of offspring survival. By aiding their daughters and raising their grandchildren, they increase the success rate of passing on their own genetic traits, which is the reason why humans are found to be fit even after their time of reproduction.

I grew up in a four-story walk-up apartment in Taipei. The family who lived above us also had a daughter my age. I see her as my alternative self had I decided to get married, have a career, and start a family in Taiwan instead of in the States. Every morning, my doppelganger likely returns to her childhood home to drop off her daughter before going to work. I heard her father is an especially doting grandparent who loves spending all day with his grandchild.

In the land of the free, I drop off my child at daycare each morning. Rosie spends her days with the maximum number of kids based on the teacher-to-student ratio. I'm not quite sure what she does all day, other than picking up germs from other children. This arrangement costs me over $400 per week.

Finding childcare is a big thing for American mothers. My Taiwanese counterpart has default childcare built into her life: two sets of grandparents to choose from. I had to start the search from scratch by trying to figure out which expensive set of strangers I should entrust my baby to.

Without extended family nearby, a new mother will also need to learn everyday childcare on her own. By the time you have certain things figured out, your kids are ready to fly the coop and your knowledge may be obsolete.

Here in the States, I've known grandparents who practically run their children's house (from grocery shopping to cooking to cleaning to childcare, plus laundry and packing lunches for the adults), but they are far and few between. There are many parents with family members who are willing to step in for childcare for short durations, a few weeks to a few months, and this time can be used to scout out affordable childcare options outside the house.

Regardless if you pay for childcare or if you stay at home to care for your kids, this is a cost that cannot be ignored. The USDA report has a specific disclaimer that it does not include the cost of lost wages because that would make the total cost of raising a child truly epic.

While the cost of childcare is a cultural and political issue here in the United States, I do have certain recommendations on managing your career while you have young children at home (see Chapter 5: More Time) that I hope are helpful.

When my husband and I were planning to have a baby, I did a lot of searching on the Internet and saw the same high figures on raising a child. It was discouraging. We were already examining our bills, trying to cut down on spending wherever possible. It felt ridiculous that we were switching to store-brand toilet paper to save a few pennies and deliberating on having a baby that will cost thousands of dollars at the same time. I fantasized that if we didn't have a baby this year, then I could finally justify getting that vintage Kelly bag. Alas, even though my calculations were sound, Jeff refused to buy into that logic. I consoled myself with the thought that a baby is a more versatile accessory anyway (you can hold it while wearing anything).

During my pregnancy, we were introduced to a whole new world of baby products. Entire new categories of goods and services appeared out of nowhere and were aggressively advertised as crucial to the well-being of our family. As I was starting from scratch in this game of "build your complete set of baby essentials," I was very overwhelmed and confused most of the time.

I remember looking at colorful mobiles for over an hour, only to remember that I had decided not to get a crib.

I didn't want to get a crib. A crib belongs in a pastel-colored room, often referred to as "the nursery." According to many online sources, this "nursery" should also have an adult-sized chair, with the changing table and baby dresser being optional. The useful life of a nursery is just over twelve months, when a baby becomes limber enough to climb out of a crib. The entire concept blew my mind—you mean I need to temporarily repurpose an entire room if I get a crib?

Who needs a crib when we have dresser drawers? I clearly

remembered reading somewhere that the Vikings put their babies in open dressers . . . or was that the Dutch . . . ?

"You can't put your baby in a dresser." My sister was exasperated that she had to explain something so simple.

Oh yes I can, I argued silently in my head. *I'll put a few blankets down first so the bottom would be comfortable. I bet I can also attach that cute crib mobile from Etsy to the side of the dresser drawer.*

My mother-in-law finally solved the problem by bringing over a bassinet, ending all arguments about whether it was kosher to use existing bedroom furniture in lieu of a crib.

A friend of mine has always been a phenomenal bargain hunter. In her pre-baby days, she had a room dedicated to clothes and always dressed fabulously. After her son was born, he became the recipient of her talent. I visited their house once and was pulled in by the complete Thomas the Tank Engine display in the center of their living room. They had mini-indoor playgrounds when he was a toddler, after which those were replaced by child-size teepees.

The trick, my friend had imparted, was part discount sales, part "buy-nothing" groups, but mainly visiting large consignment sales events that happen a few times a year.

She took me to a consignment sale once. It was a two-day event, housed in a local gymnasium. All items were for babies and toddlers only, ranging from clothes to books to toys. And, boy, was there a lot of things. Racks of clothes placed side-by-side, extending to over fifty feet each. Half a dozen folding tables stacked with enough books to rival a library. Toys of every kind imaginable. Looking for strollers? There were about twenty. High chairs? Same story.

I walked around rather dazed. There was so much *stuff* that I didn't even know where to start looking. Perhaps Rosie needs some new clothes? There were probably fifty articles of dresses, shirts, and pants her size, all neatly arranged, some with price tags still attached. Maybe I should bring home some books? There were so many volumes on the table they had to be arranged with only the spine side facing up. All in great condition.

Who needed all these things? A stadium worth, to be exact, all barely used. And who bought them to begin with? I walked out, buying nothing, and feeling confused about the experience.

You want to be well equipped with the essentials of raising a child and know that anything beyond that list is optional. Walking into retail stores or consignment shops without a clear idea of what you own or what essentials you need, like I did, would probably not save you money. Had I bought anything on that trip, most likely I would not have gotten much use out of it. I would have ended up selling or donating extra items, and they would have ended up back on the shelves of a future consignment shop. Thus, completing a cycle where the only difference would be my lighter wallet.

In the Crosshairs

New parents are establishing new shopping patterns and are less price sensitive. Marketers have known this for quite a while, which is why they make it a point to keep track of this data in order to send out ads at the right time. This is not limited to baby-related goods; life with a newborn is hectic, and mothers generally are willing to spend more for anything that may help their decision-making process while shopping.

"The companies and brands around you are being very strategic about how they can build a relationship with you or keep their existing relationship with you at this moment of flux," said Professor Karthikeya Easwar of Georgetown University McDonough School of Business when I interviewed him on how companies market to new parents.

Dr. Easwar explained that the key word is "transition." Whether you are eighteen and going to college, twenty-three and starting your first job, or at the start of parenthood, that is the moment where companies try to capture your attention to "catalyze the consumption process for a consumer."

A company's marketing effort begins when you recognize that there is a problem or change in your life. For example, you are pregnant, and your house is not properly furnished to house a baby.

"And so, when you see that gap, that's the motivator that pushes a consumer to look into the marketplace for what will close the gap," said Dr. Easwar. "The key, in essence, for any company is that a consumer needs to see a gap."

Companies then present you with an ideal solution: an artisan-crafted crib, made from natural wood, its design inspired by the movement of gentle ocean waves. The product photo shows the crib in a nursery, minimally furnished to evoke a sense of serenity. It can also be converted into a child's bed, demonstrating long-lasting value.

While you need a crib eventually, you probably don't need this crib right now.

I did a search online and found a basic crib for $135, mattress included. The artisan crib is advertised for $750. Yet, as I stare at the product photo, with its beige wood spindles, its curved edges, I realize it's a work of art, and I begin to wonder whether Rosie can still fit into it as a toddler bed.

"Marketing companies are eager to figure out how our brains work, the better to sell us everything," wrote Abigail Tucker in her book *Mom Genes*.[9]

So why is this a bad thing? Is it so terrible to be shown ads that may be timely and relevant? Of course not. Marketing, when done well, is beneficial to both seller and buyer. The real problem is the messaging of these advertisements.

There is also a long-term concern here. While we may want to spend a few more dollars to solve an immediate issue at hand (say, shop at a local grocery store when it's 11:00 p.m. and you're out of diapers), your cost of living rises if this higher-cost shopping pattern becomes a habit.

View marketing messages clearly and be conscious of forming new buying habits when becoming a parent.

The takeaways are:

- View marketing messages clearly—These ads are selling an item while displaying a lifestyle. Buying the item will not bring you that lifestyle, nor do marketers have an obligation to include an ounce of reality in these ads.
- Be conscious of new habits—Make a mental note to examine these behaviors at a later date and switch back to lower-cost options.

Enough Is Not Too Little

In America, there is a wide range of income levels. At every income level, there are mothers with the same needs. This means there are a variety of price points available for these needs.

This is not news to you. You most likely have already considered what price point provides the highest value for the lowest cost or have established certain brand loyalty. However, your baby or child does not consider this. Your baby does not care about his sense of style nor have an opinion on name brand versus store brand.

In fact, there are companies selling essentials at below cost. See the story about the stroller. The opposite is also true. Sky's the limit, and you will be spending more than $300,000 on child rearing.

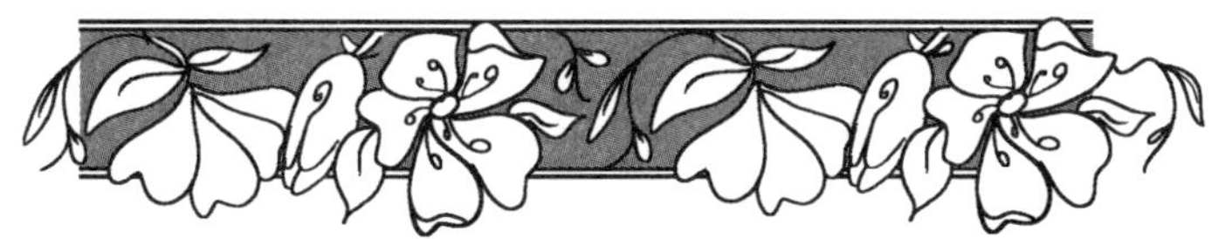

CHAPTER 7

More Money—Part 2

How much will your child's education cost?

I remember seeing an advertisement years ago that said, "Don't let your child lose at the starting line." The ad was for a fancy preschool; the text was accompanied by happy little well-dressed children engaging with blocks. Next to them was a young woman with serene countenance, looking on encouragingly.

The idea that kids who can barely walk and talk at the same time could lose to their peers was a bit of a shock. Is that even possible? And yet I remembered making a mental note to never let that happen to my child.

Very few parents have an educational strategy set for their children. Whenever I ask parents what they are doing for their child's education, the answers are about the same. Their kids are attending the local school, with afternoon sports, plus some additional extracurricular activities. Occasionally, I hear parents opt for private K-12 schools or a different public school further down the road. Sometimes special tutors are involved if the parents feel a child is not hitting their development milestones or having trouble in class. All of this results in extra expenses and *a lot* of driving.

Behind all the kerfuffle is the desire for our children to have a happy and learned childhood, with the ultimate goal of getting into the best college possible, perhaps even getting scholarships. All the while we are worried about being able to afford the ever-increasing college tuition.

Four years at a state university costs over $100,000 today. An elite private university will cost over $300,000 before your child's graduation day. And all of this is the expense *per child.*

This insane price tag plus the long runway from now until your child goes to college is the reason why we throw our hands up in despair.

Compare that to the weekly music lessons you're sending your child to at the moment. These lessons are affordable, they're something you can offer your child right now, and, who knows, maybe your child is a modern Mozart in the making. At the very least, you will be giving your child an appreciation for music for life. Doesn't that make the minor cost and inconvenience worthwhile?

Let's take a closer look at these lessons. Specifically, I want to tackle two aspects: affordability and availability. Since instructors' fees are paid based on their expertise, affordable lessons may mean that you're getting introductory classes by someone with general-level knowledge in the field. Available means that the classes are commonly offered anywhere, which also means those are likely ones that all kids are taking.

Think about the future when your child applies to college and you realize that these extracurricular activities may be the exact ones that other applicants are listing as well. We end up with a lot of minorly accomplished kids, yet all of them worked so hard for years for the sake of adding these things to their college applications.

Even more interesting is how we guide our children after they are accepted to college. Many parents I spoke to let their kids choose their own major, essentially giving them full responsibility for how that $100,000 to $300,000 is spent.

To give credit where it's due, many young adults these days are very thoughtful about how to maximize their college years so they can be productive after graduation. They are also far more vocal when the status quo does not work for them.

But we're getting ahead of ourselves . . . let us focus on your children and put together an educational strategy that will serve them without breaking the bank.

Requirements and Framework

Imagine your child in their twenties. They are fully grown (even though in your mind they'll always be just a baby), living an independent life. What is this life like? How do they spend their time? Who are they with and how is their own home life?

We want our children to have a productive life—work that is meaningful to them that at least pays the bills. We would like them to be surrounded by trusted friends. And, regardless of where and how they live, we want them to be in an environment that is challenging while staying physically safe.

This section provides a framework rather than straightforward advice. Advice is telling you what to do and in the best way that will bring you to a successful outcome. Because this is both a very personal issue with years of runway, specific advice would not be helpful. A framework demonstrates how to consider the problem so you can design a solution for yourself. Below, I offer a framework for how to set your child up for a successful life:

Framework

The desired outcome: happy and productive children for the long run

- Interpretation:
  - **Happiness** = do what you love → mostly dependent on oneself
  - **Productiveness** = make money or serve society → a match between personal skills and societal requirements

- How to get there: Focus on two or more passion/skills to train over a long period of time. Maximize ways to pay for formal education.

Why Develop Two or More Skills

Having two viable skills makes you a rare double jeopardy without having to be an expert in either of them. This advantage provides you with more options as well. However, too many passions or skill sets dilute the focus on any given one, and the end result will be just above average overall.

Calculating the Cost of Attending College for Your Child

The average cost of college in the US is $35,550 per student per year.[1] If you talk to a financial advisor, they will tell you that ideally you should start saving for that now. Realistically, I think parents will probably start saving for that when their children are in grade school (i.e., grade one, age five). My basis for that assumption is that before grade school, your child is in daycare or you're paying for some sort of childcare if you are working full time. Alternatively, if you are caring for your child, then you may be considering returning to the workforce around that time. Either way, this hopefully means that your family will have some additional money, should you consider starting a college fund for your kid.

Let's take a look at a cost-benefit analysis of this investment. Our assumptions are:

- Your child is currently five years old.
- You would like to save for full tuition and living expenses, all four years, by the time your child goes to college.
- Inflation is assumed to be at 3 percent. At the time of this writing, US inflation is around 5 percent. The Federal Reserve (the US central banking system that sets our nation's interest rates) would like it to be at 2 percent, so 3 percent is a fair assumption.
- College tuition increases at a rate of 8 percent each year.[2]
- Today's saving's return rate can also be estimated at 7 percent. This number is widely used (and I'll provide backup later).

This means that, when your child enters college at the age of eighteen, the total cost of college tuition will be $435,66.[3]

$435,663 = first year cost ($96,683) + second year cost ($104,417) + third year cost ($112,771) + fourth year cost ($121,792).

The figures listed above are based on annual tuition of $35,550 growing at a rate of 8 percent per year.

Note that these are non-inflation-adjusted figures.

What we want to know is this: how much money will you need to save each year in order to reach that goal when your child turns eighteen, assuming that your investment rate of return is 7 percent per year and inflation is 3 percent per year? I've calculated this figure using the assumptions above, and it is this: **you will have to put away $21,500 per year in order to reach this goal.**

This is a fairly crazy goal, considering that the average US household income is just over $70,000.

Let's turn this calculation around and see exactly what the impact of your saving is if you are putting away just a little money each year.

Say you can contribute $200 per month toward your child's college fund (all assumptions above still hold true). When your child turns eighteen, you will have saved over $45,000 total. This is about half a year of college tuition and board (one year will be over $90,000).

Parents' Focus on Education

Today's parents put a significant weight on paying for children's education. Starting from a young age, toddlers are put into expensive Montessori schools. This pressure continues to mount, both financially on the parents' side and emotionally on the children's side. All in hopes of getting into one of the top universities.

It is very difficult not to get sucked into the spirit of the race. One day when I went to pick up my daughter Rosie, I ran into Carter's mother. Rosie and Carter are just a month apart in age and have been in the same class up to this point. Carter ran over, showing his mother that he can now write his name.

Carter was three, and this was a pretty impressive achievement at that age. Rosie can recognize letters, but we never pushed her to write any letters, let alone her name. I always thought it was a silly thing to train kids—your name is the one thing you will not lack an opportunity to practice writing throughout your life. But right there, when I saw how proud Carter's mother was, I almost wavered and was going to march Rosie right back home to practice her letters.

But I didn't. And the reason is this: our society and its view on higher education are changing, and it is hard to predict what will be the best strategy to set our kids up for success in the future.

Taiwan's Employment Situation as an Indicator of Potential Future

In 1948 and 1949, Chiang Kai-Shek's army suffered decisive losses against the communists, and the government retreated to Taiwan. Thousands of refugees followed, abandoning families and possessions in order to start a new life. My grandmother was among the refugees.

Her siblings described her as the smartest among them. My grandmother was in her second year in college when the war broke out. It was rare for families to send their daughters to get an education at that time. Indeed, she never forgot this lost opportunity. Her only possession when she got to the port was a bolt of fabric, and she traded it for a ticket on the boat to go to Taiwan. Once she landed, she was penniless and alone.

Grandma remembers seeing a "Help Wanted" sign for a dishwasher position. This job did not interest her at first. She came from a military family with generations of history. Her family owned a large farm, she had some of the highest marks in high school, and she was going to college. But this was all left in mainland China, and she took the dishwashing post the next day. My grandmother did not stay as a dishwasher for long. A friend referred her to work at the Taiwanese Mint shortly after, and she worked there until her retirement at the age of sixty-two.

Because of this, my grandmother always put an incredible weight on education for my father. While most children had to help around the house or the family business, my father remembered growing up with the single responsibility of studying. Indeed, most of Grandma's paychecks seem to have gone into my father's well-being, so he could focus on his schoolwork.

"I always thought I was a real street fighter," my father reminisced. "Then I realized I was winning fights only because I was the only kid wearing shoes."

Dad was at the top of his class in both middle school and

high school. His entrance exam score allowed him to participate in the top major (medicine) at the top university (National Taiwan University). He graduated and became a surgeon.

Now, over seventy years old, he is still working.

"I pity the young generation of doctors now," he said. "There was no competition when I graduated. My classmates and I enjoyed long careers and had time to rise to the top of our fields.

"Young doctors now are fighting for scraps. Not only are the older doctors keeping the best cases, but there are also more new doctors competing at the bottom."

When my father was growing up, the Taiwanese education offered two paths to high school students: trade school or university. Attending a trade school was seen as a solid option. Students would start shifting their focuses in the last two years of high school, graduate earlier than university students, and start working right away. My father once calculated that it took him over ten working years to surpass the total salary of his peers who had chosen the trade school route.

As Taiwan's economy grew, participation in trade school shrank. Parents wanted their children to go to universities for the prestige. It was also the ideal way to start a successful career. What parents did not count on was the large number of college and university graduates all competing for the same jobs. Today, college graduates are going straight to graduate schools, basically doubling down on their educational investment in order to differentiate themselves to employers. There are concerns that this trend may grow until students are staying in school to obtain a PhD before joining the workforce.

The Situation in the United States

In the United States, the situation is a little different. While boomers (born between 1946 and 1964) graduated from college and were able to find stable jobs paying a living wage with health benefits, this is not the case for Gen X and millennials. Gen X (born between 1965 and 1979) and millennials (born between 1980 and 1996) both followed the boomers' steps by going to college, but these generations faced global economic crises at critical times of their lives. The Great Recession of 2008 to 2009 and the very recent 2020 pandemic made stable employment significantly rarer for Gen X and millennials when each were joining the workforce.

I illustrated the economic situation in Taiwan earlier for comparison reasons. The similarity is that a college degree is now worth less to employers. But there are some important differences:

- College education is free in Taiwan
- Health care is free in Taiwan
- There is an accepted culture of living at home until marriage in Taiwan

In other words, Taiwanese have a safety net that is not available to Americans.

How to cope with this financial situation is for a different book. What I would like to focus on in this book is thinking about spending for your child's future.

Earlier in this chapter, I calculated the amount of money a parent will have to save per year in order to pay for the rising cost of college education. An impossible amount for most income levels. I also showed that blindly increasing the level of education (like what the Taiwanese are doing now) is both unsustainable and more costly for Americans (more costly because the American government is not subsidizing education or healthcare for its people).

So why are new parents paying for expensive early childhood education? Do parents truly believe toddlers educated using expensive wooden blocks will outperform their peers in fifteen years, or are they blindly following the trend of preparing their children for college earlier and earlier?

An Alternative to the Rat Race

In his book, *Family Inc.*, Douglas McCormick provides an alternative use of wealth to jump-start your children's financial security.[4] In his example, the parents would save up to $100,000 to be given to their heir at the age of twenty-five. If the parents further held that money in savings until their heir turns forty-five (at this point, we'll use the word heir since only a parent can consider a forty-five-year-old adult as "child"), the $100,000 would have compounded to $225,000.

This is a sizable amount to start a business (any type of local business such as plumbing or dry-cleaning). A well-run business can expect a 24 percent compounded after-tax annual return. Therefore, when the heir turns sixty-five, the heir's family will have a net worth of almost nine million dollars.

Yes, a lot of things will have to go right for McCormick's heir. But a lot of things will have to go right for your child if you are following the default college track. At the end of the college track, your child will still be hard-pressed to have nine million by retirement.

Today's parents put significant weight on sending their children to college. If that is the end goal, you (as a parent) will be doing two things: putting away buckets of money for college tuition and trying to make sure your child has a glowing college application. As a result, you and your family will be spending about a decade trying to manage those two things—working hard at your job so you can save money, signing up for all the extracurricular activities for your children, and shuttling them to these activities . . . etc.

College does not provide the same guarantee as it used to. Parents should make a conscious decision on whether this is the path they want to take before expending all those resources.

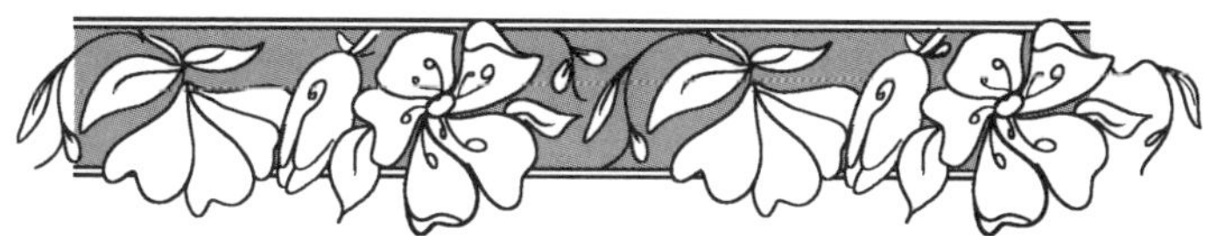

CHAPTER 8

More Energy

It was 8:00 p.m., and Rosie was happily watching TV. I saw she had already worn out my husband, who was now quietly dozing next to her. Occasionally, Rosie would nudge her daddy, trying to get his attention to watch a funny bit of the show with her. Or she would jump up and down on the sofa then climb over him like he was a part of the furniture.

How does this child have so much energy? I wondered.

In an ideal world—where parents sit down with pediatricians to discuss a child's sleeping needs and the child magically adheres to said schedule—Rosie would be bathed, changed into her jammies, would have brushed her teeth, and I would be tucking my sleepy angel in bed right about now. Alas, this vision was far from the current reality. Instead, my husband and I would spend the next forty-five minutes negotiating with Rosie on going to bed. No bath, perhaps not even changing to pj's, a half-hearted attempt at teeth brushing, and, if we're lucky, she would be content to jump on her bed by herself until she falls asleep.

By the time we closed her bedroom door, it was just past 9:00 p.m. and I was exhausted. The tiredness I felt was on par with the time I pulled an all-nighter with my consulting team, trying to answer some last-minute comments from the client. In the case of the client presentation, I got to wake up in a hotel in Madrid, had cafe con leche and *churros con chocolate* for breakfast, before making the recommendation for our client to look into Papua New Guinea for their battery storage enterprise expansion. Now, I wake up to receive a hug and a kiss from my daughter, offer her a variety of breakfast choices (all of which she will inevitably refuse . . . a good eater, she is not), before changing her clothes (so nobody would know she had no bath last night) and ushering her to daycare. Although the joy I feel on seeing my daughter every morning is comparable to nailing a client presentation, the rest of the world would probably value (and reward) the latter more.

If childcare was less exhausting, we could accomplish more—have children and eat the *churro con chocolate* too.

There was a moment when I thought, *Enough is enough*. I could not keep running myself ragged, day in and day out. It was 11:00 p.m. No dishes were washed, no laundry folded. The kitchen and living room remained the mess they were at the start of the evening. I had been sitting in front of the TV, binging Netflix for the past two hours. And still I didn't want to go to bed.

"We're at home, burned out after a long day . . . We put the kids to bed; we caught up on email. We're so exhausted it feels like all we can do is just veg out on the couch . . . when in fact, we need one final push of discipline: picking ourselves up and walking to the bedroom and passing out . . . It will solve so many of your problems."

—Ryan Holiday, *Discipline Is Destiny*

In his book *Discipline Is Destiny: The Power of Self-Control*, Ryan Holiday wrote:

> *We're at home, burned out after a long day . . . We put the kids to bed; we caught up on email. We're so exhausted it feels like all we can do is just veg out on the couch . . . when in fact, we need one final push of discipline: picking ourselves up and walking to the bedroom and passing out . . . It will solve so many of your problems.*

That "final push of discipline" takes energy. I knew that if I could manage my day in a way that left me that small ounce of power, then I could haul my body to bed and kick off the virtuous cycle of waking up more refreshed.

Finding more energy for parents has a two-part solution:

- Address the energy drain when we are with our kids, and
- Improve general energy management in our daily lives.

Managing Our Energy

My husband and I had a courtship that was spent mostly in front of the TV. After getting through the customary coffee and dinner dates, we realized both of us are homebodies with a fondness for watching anime. To an outsider, it may appear that we were determined to have a lifetime of conversation topics based on shows before we would commit to tying the knot.

Even after we were married, we continued to bond over shows. Our guilty pleasure went more mainstream, and there was a lot of time spent watching *The Great British Baking Show*. After both working for a full day, we would have dinner, spend some time tidying the house, then settle in with a bottle of beer and a glass of wine and go through a couple episodes each evening.

This routine changed when we first brought Rosie home from the hospital. For the first few months, we were just trying to get our bearings. We needed both incomes, and there were many discussions with each of our managers regarding work schedules and responsibilities.

One thing we held steadfast throughout the first year of becoming parents was our TV-watching habit. It appears crazy to me now that I was waking up two, three times a night, night after night, but still insisted on staying up to watch an hour-long show on most days. It seems crazy that I changed almost everything about my daily schedule except this. These shows added no value to my work or to my personal growth, but it was really hard for me to let go. My husband and I bonded over television. It was the only entertainment we had on most days, as well as the only source of conversation topics that didn't revolve around housework and childcare.

What finally made me change this behavior was when I decided that I wanted a promotion. While my manager was extremely understanding and helped me reshape my workload into something manageable, it came at a cost. There was an unspoken agreement that I would never get a promotion again in this new role. I would be the steady rock of the team, working the same job, providing stability, allowing others to rotate in and out of the team as they ascended in their careers.

It was a reasonable trade-off, at first. I was overwhelmed at everything I had to learn at home about being a mother, I couldn't imagine ever needing more stress at work ever again. It seems silly that I didn't consider the fact that babies grow up to be toddlers, toddlers grow up to be children, and at every stage there is less dependence on the mother. Nor did I think about how boring a job can get after doing the same thing, day in and day out, after a few years.

I returned to my manager once more, around the time Rosie turned two, and asked for a promotion. This request received a "we'll consider it (i.e. highly unlikely to happen)" response. I looked around to find a way to increase my value at work and decided that I should get my CPA certification. Long story short, I started waking up at 5:00 a.m. each morning in order to study for the exams. And to accommodate this new wake time, I finally gave up my late-night TV-watching habit.

Our body's natural energy rhythm throughout the day is regulated by the circadian system. The circadian rhythm is an internal biological clock and influences much of our physiological and behavioral processes.

In the early morning, many people experience a natural

increase in energy alertness. This is due to an increase of cortisol after waking. Cortisol is also referred to as the "stress hormone." It helps our body wake up in the morning and prepare for the day ahead.

Our alertness usually sustains over the course of the morning. After lunch, our body redistributes blood flow to focus on digestion, giving us that post-lunch dip that can last for two hours.[1]

Energy returns in the early afternoon. From late afternoon until evening, there may be a steady decline as we wrap up the day. As daylight fades, our melatonin level rises to help us prepare for sleep.

To manage your energy, start by creating time brackets for your twenty-four-hour period:

- Morning Peak (6:00–9:00 a.m.)
- Late Morning (9:00 a.m.–12:00 p.m.)
- Afternoon Dip (1:00–3:00 p.m.)
- Afternoon Recovery (3:00–6:00 p.m.)
- Evening Wrap-up (6:00–9:00 p.m.)
- Nighttime Relaxation (9:00–11:00 p.m.)
- Nighttime Sleep (11:00 p.m.–6:00 a.m.)

Consider this as the baseline for everyone. While some of us would like to label ourselves as either a morning lark or a night owl, these are more attributed to habits rather than differences in biological programming. It is unlikely that your body's function differs greatly from the typical human being.

If you are satisfied with the energy level you routinely have, that is great. This means your current lifestyle supports your goals and that is always cause for celebration. If you would like to make some adjustments, read on.

Start with the typical energy rhythm listed above. As you can see, it divides up the day into three-hour segments. Starting from your wake time, make minor adjustments to get to your customized energy rhythm. For example, if you wake up at 7:00 a.m. each day instead of 6:00, push the time brackets back by an hour so you'll have morning peak from 7:00 a.m. to ten a.m., late morning from 10:00 a.m. to 1:00 p.m., etc. Make further adjustments with the times you typically have lunches and dinners. Meals have a big impact on our energy level. For example, afternoon dip should start after your lunch time. If you don't finish lunch until 2:00 p.m., then push back the afternoon dip bracket to 2:00 p.m. to 4:00 p.m. If each of your customized brackets is not three hours long, that is okay too.

Next step, map your daily schedule to your customized energy rhythm. Is there a typical time you take your kids to daycare or school? A certain time you get in and out of the office? More specifically, are there standard tasks or meetings you perform daily? Mark the time of these activities into each of your energy brackets.

Consider what you have now. You should be able to see

which daily activities are currently occupying which energy bracket. Check whether you are using your energy efficiently. For example, unless you are caring for children full time, child-care tasks should not be placed into the prime energy spots, such as the morning or early afternoon.

See if you can rearrange your schedule so the tasks requiring the highest focus are matching your prime energy level. Many of us who work in the office have a habit of checking emails first thing in the morning. This may not be the most efficient use of your energy. You may want to put off checking your email until late afternoon and use the morning to get tasks requiring a high level of concentration and creativity done.

Try to stick to this new schedule, as repeating the same behavior daily will let your body know that this is the new status quo moving forward.

Many others with small children that I have interviewed told me that they are waking up early, even though this wasn't a habit before they became mothers. Most are waking up between 5:00 and 6:00 a.m. to do more. This is referred to as the "quiet time" before the rest of the household wakes up.

While there are other ways to boost your energy, such as a better diet and exercise or adding stimulants (e.g., coffee), personally, I believe changing your routine is a more effective way for mothers—this is a no-cost and no additional long-term commitment strategy.

Managing Our Children's Energy

Let's face it, while we hate having no fuel left for ourselves at the end of each day, this is still a good problem to have. If we were babysitting mannequins, we wouldn't have had an energy drain problem. We have inquisitive, vivacious children with little idea of the limitations of the world—and that's a good thing.

When Michaeleen Doucleff was researching parenting theories of our ancestors, she traveled to a Mayan village in the Yucatan Peninsula with her small daughter, also named Rosie. The Doucleffs received a warm welcome from the locals and lived with one of the families for a short time. During that time, Michaeleen saw that her daughter's behavior was different. Rosie was more cooperative while with the Mayan family, less prone to tantrums when compared to traveling with just Michaeleen.

Michaeleen suspected this was due to the amount of control American parents—i.e. herself—try to exert on their children.

From the day our children are born, we have high expectations for them. The baseline of these expectations is that they will grow up in our society and live productive lives. In America, this mostly translates to being a good eater, a good sleeper, playing well with others, and being curious and kind. For ambitious parents, we probably would like our children's learning to excel as well.

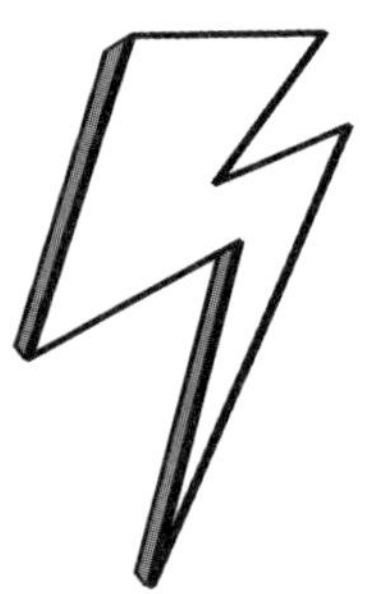

Source of Parental Expectations

I found a document from the District of Columbia Public Schools website titled "Family Guide to Kindergarten Readiness Standards."[2] The guide listed eight separate areas a child is to be evaluated around the age of five when they are to enter the public school system. While many of the development milestones are universal to children anywhere—for example, following directions, the ability to describe oneself and their family, or basic controls of arms and legs (basic "gross motor skills") and hands and feet ("fine motor skills")—there is also a list of requirements for language and literacy, mathematical thinking, science, social studies, and creative arts.

Once parents start thinking about academic excellence for their children, then there really is no limit to our expectations. There is always another child genius around the block, always something else we want to teach them.

My Story

Being born and raised in Taiwan, I am fluent in both English and Mandarin. It is an unspoken expectation for Chinese parents to teach their children to speak Chinese. Therefore, I spent the first few years of Rosie's life speaking every sentence in two languages—first in Chinese, and whenever she looked at me in confusion, I would repeat myself again in Chinese slowly, then I would finally give up and say what I wanted to say in English.

If you've ever had to listen to someone speaking to you in slow and deliberate tones in a foreign language, then you'd know that it is pretty annoying. I'd attest that it's equally frustrating on the speaker's part. Rosie often looked at me blankly or ignored me altogether. This created a lot of anxiety for me—my daughter was going to grow up not knowing how to identify cats and dogs in Chinese, all due to my incompetence.

To avoid that total catastrophe, I bought Chinese learning tools. Flash cards and exercise books, along with downloading videos of cartoon characters, also speaking in very slow and deliberate Mandarin, made for American-born Chinese children. I looked for Chinese schools near our home, which held classes every Friday afternoon. The entire effort was more than a little taxing. Moreover, we would have to pay for the extra schooling and lose a few hours each week from now until years into the foreseeable future.

Finally, my sister pulled me aside one day and asked, "Why are you doing this? We don't know any Chinese families here and you don't even enjoy speaking Mandarin. When the time comes, Rosie can learn Chinese. Until then, you should really give it a break."

So I did. The amazing thing was that Rosie and I started exchanging meaningful words from the day when I switched to speaking to her in English only. It was as if I never actually tried to listen to her when I was forcing two languages into our conversations.

Today, Rosie speaks no Chinese. Zilch. However, she does have excellent enunciation in English and a large vocabulary for her age. We have Fridays all to ourselves, and, most importantly, we understand every word we speak to each other, always.

You need to decide your own philosophy for your children's education. Without conscious planning and deliberate execution, our society will push your child toward excelling at all topics. While learning is a privilege, you must be careful to choose subjects which your child enjoys and what works for your family's lifestyle. If you and your partner are self-proclaimed tone-deaf, does it really make sense for your child to have the same training schedule as Mozart? Perhaps just a few music appreciation lessons would suffice.

Children Mimicking Our Behavior + Requiring Extra Time for Them to Calm Down

Another area of energy management is during our interaction with our children. Many experts recommend play as a form of conflict resolution with children.[3,4] Play is an excellent way to redirect focus and connect with our children. It brings joy and laughter, which is what we strive for, not only in our kids' lives but in our own as well. What I find missing from these expert instructions is how to calm our children down after the play is over.

I walked into the living room one day after hearing peals of laughter and saw that my husband, for some reason, decided to pick my daughter up and hold her upside down. Rosie found her situation hilarious, and both father and daughter were giggling unstoppably.

"Whew . . . okay, that's enough, I think," my husband said, after gently setting our daughter down. Rosie spent a few minutes recovering on the floor, catching her breath. Then she jumped up excitedly, "Catch me, Daddy! You can't catch me!"

I could see the dismay on Jeff's face. "Now Rosie, I think we should stop . . . let's play something else."

That request fell upon deaf ears. Rosie just kept yelling, "Come on, Daddy, come on!"

Calming an overexcited child is one of the hardest things for parents. Whether the overexcitement is due to play (like my husband's case) or situational (many times we refer to that as throwing a tantrum), there is something to keep in mind that would help with the situation.

Children's Big Emotions

Children have big emotions and are still learning to regulate them. As adults, we are more adept at understanding and managing our emotions. We understand that both happy and sad moments pass. They are just a small part of life, and we don't see the need to dwell on them. For kids, many of their experiences are brand new—too exciting to resist or too upsetting to handle.

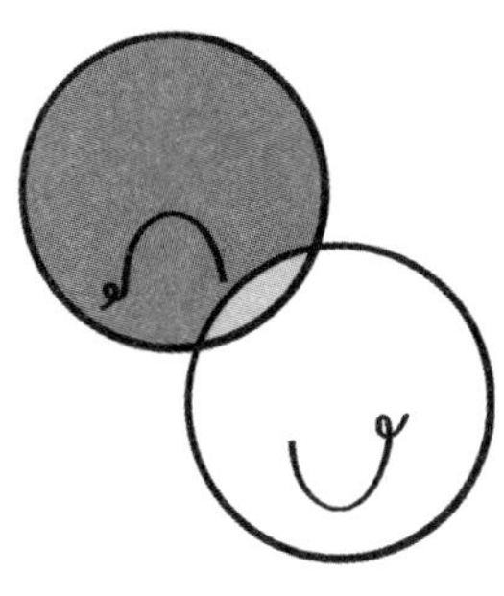

Imagine you are whisked away to Bolivia on a journey to see the Uyuni Salt Flat, one of the most spectacular sights on earth. The desert-like land stretches as far as the eye can see. It rained the night before, and there is a thin layer of water that covers the dried-up lake, producing a breathtaking mirror effect. Words cannot describe the sight before you, and you are awestruck at its majesty. Then your tour guide says, "Okay, that's enough, I think. Now let's have lunch. I prepared some yummy carrot sticks for you."

How you would respond to that situation would highly depend on your personality, but it's safe to say that you probably wouldn't have a positive and compliant reaction.

Our everyday world is wondrous and amazing when viewed through the eyes of a small child. Without the aid of years of life experience, it is difficult for them to behave calmly and gracefully under all circumstances.

Next time, when you find your child overly excited, threatening to drain your energy and take away your sanity, take a moment to pause. For you, this pause is a mental reminder to check in with yourself and reset your own expectations on how long it will take to move on from the situation. For your child, while he may be physically next to you, his mind is off somewhere else—either in the pit of gloom and doom or high in the air with rainbows and unicorns. Either way, he may need a few minutes before he is ready to connect with you and the real world.

TAKEAWAYS

Managing children's energy takes time and a lot of patience, as they experience the world around us differently. Many things are novel to them, and parents often use play as a good way to connect. Combine this with kids' difficulty with emotional regulation, and we can understand that they need our help when coming down from highs.

When you're ready for your child to participate in calmer activities:

- Take a long pause
- Model the calm behavior
- Reset your expectation and connect with your child

The Generation Cycle

One of the hardest things in parenting is breaking the generation cycle. Growing up, we experienced parenting from our caretakers, and sometimes we can't help but use the same parenting techniques of the previous generation, even if we despised it.

In Taiwan, I was beaten as a child. Frequently and hard. The beating did not come from my parents but from my elementary school teachers. It was commonplace for teachers to

*In difficult moments,
give yourself grace and give your
child the gift of connecting with you.*

discipline children with sticks. While I did not misbehave, I did have poor grades, and I had one teacher who tried his very best to beat the ignorance out of me.

Even though I had suffered through that terrible experience, I thought for certain I should use corporal punishment on my daughter. Spare the rod and spoil the child, as the old saying goes. It wasn't until Rosie was born that I changed my mind. I remembered looking into her tiny face and making a promise to myself that I would never hit her, ever. It took determination to follow through, for I must admit that on the rare occasion with Rosie acting out, I thought how easy it would have been for me to give a small but firm slap on her buttocks to show her that I was serious. I held back, but it was confusing because I also didn't know what else to do.

Think about all the ways you currently interact with your child. Are there things you are doing because that was how you were raised? Perhaps your parents made you sit at the dinner table and insisted that you eat everything on the plate, and now you are also making a similar demand on your children? Talk to your pediatrician, read expert opinions on the subject, and if you discover that children can generally moderate their eating and still be healthy, then consider letting go of the expectation of having them sit through their dinner as well. Once they're full, let them go. This will save you energy at the dinner table, and it builds trust with your child so future interactions may be smoother as well.

Pareto at Work

Remember what we discussed earlier regarding the Pareto principle?

When we face a fork in the road, it is not always immediately apparent if we made the right choice.

How I Met Your Mother (HIMYM) was Cobie Smulders's big break. The show enjoyed nine successful seasons before going into indication. Smulders portrayed Robin Scherbatsky, a TV reporter and one of the five main characters.

One of the toughest decisions Smulders must have come across was when Joss Whedon offered her the starring role of Wonder Woman. This would have been a role of a lifetime. Whedon's Wonder Woman script had envisioned a witty Diana, perfectly matched with Smulders's HIMYM persona. However, becoming Wonder Woman would have pulled Smulders into the DC Universe, tying her forever to that role. The fame would also take a huge toll on her family life.

Cobie Smulders chose to become Maria Hill instead, a minor role in the Marvel Universe, and starred in two *Avenger* movies. Her appearances in these two movies were minor.

"We'll just have to see if there is more avenging to do," said Smulders in a *WIRED Autocomplete Interview*.

Maria Hill did indeed keep avenging. Cobie starred in two more *Avengers* movies as well as *Spider-Man: Far from Home*. In 2020, when Cobie was on the *Tonight Show*, Jimmy Fallen exclaimed, "You were in *Avengers*, you were in *Spider-Man*, combined, this was almost four billion [in gross earnings]."

By turning down starring as Wonder Woman, Smulders was able to be in multiple *Avengers* movies as well as a cameo in the TV series, *Agents of S.H.I.E.L.D.* She is able to have a relatively normal family life without carrying the label of Wonder Woman for many years.

The Pareto Principle states that 80 percent of your result comes from 20 percent of your work. After becoming a mother, we may look at work differently. I myself used to place work on a much more important pedestal until Rosie was born. Consider this—you can maintain 80 percent of your previous output at work but greatly reduce your workload if you can figure out which 20 percent of your time would produce that work.

TAKEAWAYS

Our biological starting point for our energy level is most likely the same. Any perceived difference may be due to our habits. While there are artificial ways of boosting our energy level, such as caffeine and other stimulants, I recommend a more natural way: by adjusting your daily schedule and utilizing the time when our bodies are naturally more alert with tasks that demand more mental attention. Another way to look at this is that we should be doing childcare and household chores outside of our prime energy slots and give ourselves the gift of a clear mind, reserving that time for the tasks we would like to accomplish for ourselves.

"Whether you think you can, or you think you can't—you're right."

—Henry Ford

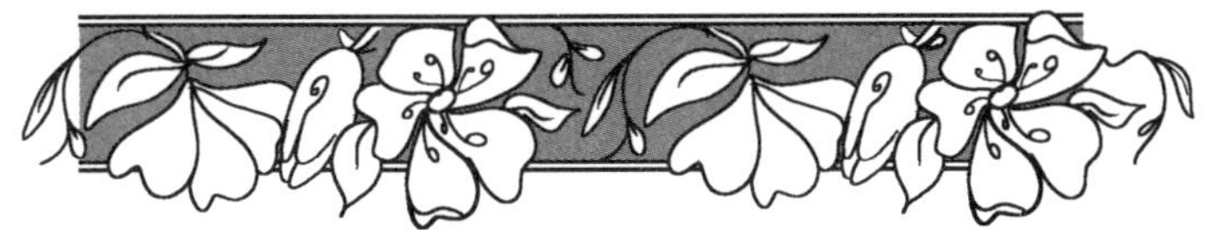

CHAPTER 9

More Space

Dictionary.com defines "peace of mind" as a mental state of calmness or tranquility, a freedom from worry and anxiety.

It is a rare mental state for mothers to come by. It is also my goal to get you closer to that tranquility, freed from worry and anxiety at all times. Whenever you find yourself unable to relax or find your mind racing when there is literally nothing you can do, the tools in this chapter will help you lay down your thoughts, smooth your emotions, and get to stillness.

Let's start with a question: What do you have to do today?

If you cannot provide a minute-by-minute account of what actions you will take, in the most efficient order, for the rest of your waking hours, then congratulations, you are human.

Researchers know there is a capacity to humans' short-term working memory.[1] Our short-term memory plays a critical role in the cognitive process—the ability to perceive, think, reason, and learn. In essence, numerous complex mental activities occur in our brains before we can take the next step. Organizing, performing, and keeping track of every step we need to make to have a functional life is, therefore, impossible to always hold in our conscious minds. Yet we still try to do it.

We try to keep shopping lists in our heads, hold imaginary conversations we would like to have with our bosses, make mental notes, berate ourselves for things that happened in the past, and worry about things yet to happen in the future. None of these thoughts that are roaming in our brains move the needle in the real world.

Below are two tracks of lessons that will help you reach calmness and serenity. One is for getting stuff done, the other is for letting thoughts go. I find I am the happiest when I am lost in a creative pursuit (such as writing), living in the moment (chatting with my husband), or daydreaming (imagining where we will go for our next vacation). If I dwell on stuff that needs to be done (chores at home, tomorrow's work) or things that happened previously (the waiter with a terrible attitude), I tend to store up negative emotions and spiral into a depressive state. Eventually, drained of all energy, I just want to go to bed so I can stop thinking about anything at all.

Getting Stuff Done

The human mind was never designed to hold as much information as we try to force it to. The things a mother needs to remember to do from dawn to dusk might go something like this:

- Check the weather to make sure Jimmy is dressed appropriately for school.
- Ask Carter's mother, if she is also at drop-off, whether she will be signing Carter up for soccer this season.
- Go through the stack of hand-me-downs from Jimmy's cousins and look for the next size up in clothing, as Jimmy just grew two inches overnight.
- Organize the garage—ha!
- Set up a meeting with another manager to discuss sharing resources on a cost-saving idea.
- Prepare for this afternoon's sales call.
- Remember to bring a sweater to the freezer cell that's referred to as "the office."
- Pick up salt in the next grocery run (seriously, who runs out of salt?!).
- Ask Louisa if there is a plumber she would recommend because the dripping sound from the bathroom is really starting to get to you.
- Tell the cleaners to skip next Thursday since the family is visiting Mema and Pop Pop for a long weekend.
- Remind the pet sitter not to overfeed Fluffy.
- Cook dinner.
- Cook backup dinner in case Jimmy absolutely refuses to eat dinner . . .

- Pick up some of that lavender-scented baby bath soap (read somewhere that helps kids fall asleep faster—really hope that works). I could use some lavender-scented bath soap myself . . .

The list goes on.

A lot of times, we may find these tasks so mundane and deem them not time worthy of writing down. This would be like taking multiple loads of dirty laundry and stuffing everything into your state-of-the-art washer without sorting or pre-treating—fine if that is what needs to be done in a pinch, but there is a more elegant way to use that washer to produce better results.

The human brain is designed to keep us alive. This starts from the most basic physiological needs of breathing, food, water, sex, and sleep. The next level is safety. Making sure ourselves and our families are not harmed, our properties are not damaged or invaded, and our work (which brings us monetary gains and maintains our social status) is secure.

The unconscious mind is keeping track of our physical surroundings and noting where something might go wrong. Today, we are not running from saber-toothed tigers anymore, but if we perceive something to be just as dangerous, then our brain

If your mind is empty, it is always ready for anything; it is open to everything.

- Shunryū Suzuki

is already wired up to deal with that danger. By keeping any incomplete task inside our heads, our minds cannot help but continue to investigate it—is it threatening? Is it opportunistic? Should I do something about it? Since we haven't properly reviewed and labeled that task, the mind labels it for us based on our initial feeling toward the uncompleted task.

What we want is to be agile, flexible, and graceful when it comes to tackling the items on our to-do list. This gives us the ability to expend the appropriate energy on each item without overblowing or undermining anything. Furthermore, when something new comes up, we would then have the mental space to deal with the new issue calmly.

Imagine you are driving down the road with that previous list of things in your head. Suddenly, a car pulls in front of you, causing you to break hard and nearly rear-end its bumper. Depending on how much mental burden you were under, this may be just the thing causing you to lose your calm.

Having an organized mind is about being in control of the nitty-gritty things in life. While we cannot control everything that happens to us—nor do I advocate for that—as mothers, we want to have a solid handle on our lives and our children's lives for the baseline stuff. That is the foundation for us to build that calmness to deal with new things that get tossed into the daily mix.

Once we get that to-do list out of our heads and to a place where our mind can trust it will eventually get done, we can be more present in our lives. So if you're driving down the road and a car pulls in front of you, causing a near-miss, you can instead take a deep breath, let out some choice curse words, then drive on. You are fine. Your life is fine. And there will be dinner on the table because you're not missing a beat because of some bozo who can't drive.

The Method, Explained

Essentially, the method is to do a thorough offload of everything you consider to be incomplete. This includes anything you've agreed to do for yourself and for others. Everything you believe to be your responsibility or burden to bear.

If your brain accepts that these thoughts are now safely stored elsewhere, then it will stop trying to revisit the issue. For example, you probably don't find yourself trying to memorize everything you try to google because you can just pull out your phone and google the question again.

Here are the steps.

Write Everything Down

While it is best to be sitting alone and comfortably while doing this, it is not a prerequisite. As long as you have enough writing paper and you can read your writing later on, that's good enough. Now, list everything that is negatively impacting your mental space. This includes your to-do list, the things you need to (or want to) say to people, your good ideas for anything you want to do in the future . . . All of them go into that list on that piece of paper.

While Dr. Sarah Knott, a professor at Indiana University, was researching motherhood history, she found many interruptions in the writings of mothers. "The mothers of infants, or indeed children under five, were terrible correspondents," Knott described.[2]

Each interruption causes a task to be stretched out due to the extra effort it takes for us to pull our focus back and resume where we had left off prior to the interruption.

If you're sitting down and doing this for the first time, this exercise can take an hour without distraction. If you keep getting pulled away, then make sure you keep your pencil and paper close by to continue writing whenever another thought pops up. You know you're done when you are looking around the room, thinking, but no longer able to come up with anything else to write.

Organize on Paper

I once had a finance professor named Vladimir. He was thin, tall, bespectacled, always suited when teaching, and spoke with a thick Russian accent. He described learning to code when growing up under the Soviet Union. Computer time was hard to come by, so the students would first write their code down on paper, run through the code mentally, and try to debug it before entering the whole thing into the computer. While this sounds time-consuming, Vladimir explained that you actually save time by laying out all of your thoughts first.

For his class, all of us had to write out our formulas on paper before typing them into Excel. Needless to say, that was not how I started my work when alone. I'd pull out my laptop and begin typing away. *There is no error in a spreadsheet that cannot be corrected quickly with just a few keystrokes*, I thought, and writing out the formula is just a waste of time.

I'd say, from a full semester of building financial models and years of experience after graduation, Professor Vlad was right. A formula as easy as "= A1 + B2" doesn't need to be pre-written. But I found that anything that requires some thinking is better when sketched out first, off of the spreadsheet. Our minds are complicated machines. We engage our minds differently when we write information out compared to just typing it (don't ask me why, I just know it's true and you should try it).

After you write down everything that is on your mind, you are ready to put some organization into the list without taking the content off the paper. Start by noting the following related information for each item:

- Time-based
- Location-based
- Person-based

Does something need to be done right now? Or can it only happen next Thursday? Those are time-based activities, and you should label their associated time down. Then there are actions that are location-based. For example, a shopping list is based on the location where the items can be purchased. There are also person-based tasks—conversations you need to have with your partner, your child, your colleagues, etc.

Once this supplementary information has been written down, you should start seeing a pattern emerge. Where to start tackling your list should become more apparent.

This organization process helps you properly allocate each item you wrote to its final destination. Time-based items should go on your calendar or planner. Location-based items should be separated out so it is clear all the actions you will need to take when physically at a certain location. Finally, for person-based items, I have a separate list for each person and append the list to my calendar based on when I will be meeting that individual.

Don't Lose the Paper

While it may sound ridiculous, I have lost this paper before. The most important part of this task is convincing your brain that there is a properly functioning system outside of itself that is taking care of organizing these tasks. If you lose the paper, your brain will continue to revisit these tasks incessantly.

More likely than losing the paper is that you will get interrupted. Between the time when you get everything out of your head and onto the paper and the time it takes to organize each item, something else will require your attention. You may have to attend a meeting or make dinner. Frankly, this is an ongoing process, and we should be prepared for interruption.

At this point, quickly pick out any items on your paper that require attention RIGHT NOW. This means between the time you put down your piece of paper and have time to pick it back up again. If you don't have time to work on your list until Friday, then you need to make sure you don't leave something on the list that needs to be done on Thursday. That action needs to live elsewhere off of your list so you can properly address it.

What you're doing here is creating a mental divider: everything that is still on the paper does not need your attention. There is a future point in time when you will revisit the list, and you can worry about all that you've written down then. But until then, those pesky tasks can live in the nebula, with no effect on you or your psyche. By creating this mental divider and building trust in this system, you can cut down your mental load effectively.

But what about the rest of the stuff on that list?

That piece of paper isn't going into the trash can. You're still going back to that list. But you're choosing the time when you do so. Instead of dealing with the items on the paper at the end of the day, when kids are asking for their snacks and you're working on getting that last email sent, you can wait until the next morning before the family is up, the house is quiet, and you have a cup of coffee in hand.

Letting Thoughts Go

There are other types of thoughts that cannot be dealt with by action. These are usually thoughts that are attached to deep emotions. Thoughts that seemingly come out of nowhere and tend to grab our attention, often dragging down our day. Let's address them here.

Ashlee was working with a lawyer. The lawyer came strongly recommended, and she was hoping for a working relationship. Her own business had been steadily growing, and she had been spending much of her energy this year on making a breakthrough for her team, hoping to bring everyone to the next level with the services she was providing to her clients.

When she received a bill from the lawyer, Ashlee was shocked. The bill was for six hundred dollars, and they had not spoken for months. Ashlee called up the lawyer and the two had an argument. "Did you not think I was going to charge you for my time?" the lawyer asked. Ashlee was dumbfounded. If she had forgotten to bill a client, she would certainly have reached out first and apologized before sending anything. But there was no apology, no explanation of the delay.

"What will you do?" I asked Ashlee.

"I'm going to pay the bill, I guess," she said. "I don't think I will be working with him now."

Ashlee was clearly exasperated. Indeed, after paying the bill and stopping her interaction with this other person, there seemed to be no other action she could take. Yet, as I was talking to her, I could tell that this particular experience was still lingering, taking up space in Ashlee's mind and expending her energy.

"Next time this thought comes up, try not to push it away immediately," I said to Ashlee.

I advised her to take a moment to examine the emotions she was experiencing and try to tease out a single emotion.

- Is it hurt?—I can't believe someone would treat me this way.
- Is it guilt?—It was my fault. I shouldn't have engaged him in the first place.
- Is it anger?—How dare he even have the guts to send that bill!

Once you name that emotion, sit with it for a minute. Really see it and validate it:

- Hurt—Of course I would feel hurt. I conducted myself properly throughout this interaction, and he responded like I was unreasonable.

- Guilt—Yes, it is reasonable to feel guilt. There is truth in the matter that I had approached him first.
- Anger—This is a valid response to such an aggravating experience!

After that, let the thought go.

The next time the thought rises up unbidden, it may be fueled with one of the other emotions. Repeat the same exercise, one emotion at a time, until the entire thought no longer impacts you.

This type of emotional work takes time. Our normal response to unpleasant thoughts is to usually beat it down with negative self-talk:

- Hurt—"Stop feeling wounded. You're stronger than that."
- Guilt—"Well it was my fault to begin with, I just need to pay the bill and walk away."
- Anger—"Being angry isn't going to solve anything, just forget about it."

This negative self-talk, while fast, does not properly address our feelings. Unaddressed feelings will continue to linger and come up unbidden. By giving time and permission to properly identify and accept ourselves, we come out of these negative experiences stronger.

Clear mental space is rare for everyone, especially for

A cup of tea, a quick stretch. Make a conscious effort to root your calmness in simpler, everyday activities.

mothers. Like our children, we are growing and experiencing new things every day. Not only do we need to have a clear mind to deal with events, this will also help us become solid role models for our kids.

A Tidy Space Is a Losing Battle

We all yearn for a clean and tidy space. The idea of minimalism is so attractive because the clearness of the space reflects the clearness we would like to have in our minds. A place for everything and everything in its place. To have only the items that we need, exactly where they ought to be when we need them. That is not how a mother's living space works.

Unless you live apart from your children, there will always be some chaos in your living space. Your kids want to explore, play, and be entertained. This involves pulling out every toy and many items that were never meant to be played with. The toys will be handled and scattered, sometimes broken but most likely never put back where they belong.

You, on the other hand, need to run a house with limited time and attention. That means laundry might be left unfolded and everyone just pulls clean but rumpled clothes from the dryer for the week. And the kitchen sink is full of dirty dishes more often than not. Occasionally, you might just want to throw caution and everything you own to the wind, drop the vacuum, and binge-watch *Bridgerton*, because, damn it, you deserve it, and all the characters are pristine-looking, and that makes you happy.

So what are we to do?

Examining our intention to have a clear space—the need for that reflection of clarity in our own minds. We can perhaps find other ways to achieve the same goal. What can we substitute in the place of a clean house that would achieve a calmness of mind? It may be sitting quietly for a few minutes with a cup of tea, closing your eyes, and letting the warm scent sooth your mind. It might be a quick yoga stretch where you let your limbs loosen and feel the tension release from your body.

When we take a walk in nature, we can see the trees and grass, all of the woodland creatures. None of them are lined up neatly or tucked away in an orderly fashion. Yet the idiosyncratic way does not bother us. We see the space as beautiful.

Let go of the idea that your living space needs to be always neat and orderly. Change your perspective and see it as the place where you nurture your family. If your children are happy, and your home is not hazardous, then perhaps that is enough.

Train your mind to use those substitutions, a cup of tea or a quick stretch, to give you the same satisfaction as having a clean house. Those are doable things within your control.

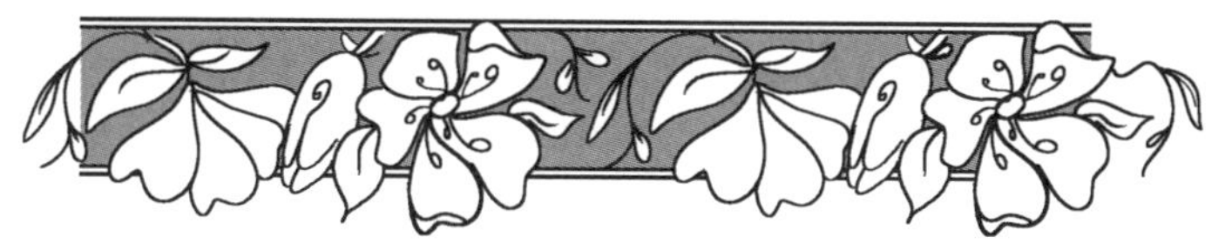

CHAPTER 10

The Growth Mindset + Learning Curriculum

This evening, unprompted, Rosie decided to clean up the living room before going to bed. She picked up the Uno cards we were playing with, carefully stacked them up, and came over to me for help putting the cards back into the card case.

"Good job!" I praised her. Then I immediately checked myself.

In 2006, psychologist Carol Dweck published her landmark book *Mindset: The New Psychology of Success*.[1] The book was tremendously successful. Shortly after its publication, *New York Magazine* issued a cover story, "How Not to Talk to Your Kids." It was one of the most-read articles for months and prompted many conversations on parenting.

According to Dweck, parents and teachers should praise children for their effort instead of the result of their work.

Personally, I cannot help praising Rosie, even if it is for

something small. I am constantly in awe of her growth abilities. Plus, I feel that children are constantly challenged to grow externally and that some praise shouldn't be harmful.

But this book is about you, not about your children.

In Dweck's words, "I wrote *Mindset* after years of research on why some people fulfill their potential and some don't. I found that one simple belief had a profound effect—whether people believed their basic traits were simply fixed . . . or were things they could develop . . . Over and over, I found that a fixed mindset held people back and a growth mindset liberated them to pursue what they valued with passion and resilience."

One of Dweck's studies examined participants' brain activities when the participants were reviewing their mistakes on a test given as part of the study. The participants who were labeled with growth mindset showed brain-processing activities, while those labeled with fixed mindset showed none.

The growth mindset became quite sensational to the general public, with some taking its application one step further to apply to children. Some fear that praising children may box them into the fixed mindset and stunt their ability to be curious or seek out challenges. Instead,

children's accomplishments should be noted, and that recognition should be praise enough on its own.

The growth mindset is characterized as the belief that one's ability to be inspired, learn, and grow is unlimited. A person with a growth mindset is said to be always stepping out of her comfort zones and seeking challenges. This attitude is said to be rewarded with personal growth, which creates a feedback loop of creating a mindset that thrives on challenge.

Sounds pretty exhausting, doesn't it?

As a mother, there are days when I feel like a bag of bones, wrapped by a donut of fat, tattooed in a layer of stretch marks. Days when the only thing I can do is vegging out on the sofa because I don't even have the willpower to get through the self-care tasks for getting in bed.

However, that is not every day.

More importantly, I don't want that to be every day of my life until Rosie grows up and leaves the house. There are many things I want to accomplish now.

Watching my child as she grows is one of the most amazing parts of motherhood for me. I can now understand why many people describe children as sponges, just soaking up the information. But if we step back, we can perhaps see the children's surrounding environment that helps them to grow.

Each morning, I put a plate of breakfast in front of Rosie after she wakes up (she doesn't always eat it). Then she has a full day at pre-K with a set learning curriculum and a group of kids her age she interacts with. She has a teacher monitoring her learning and makes corrections and gives her advice. She runs around outside. When she comes home, she watches educational programs or shows designed to stretch her imagination. I put another plate of food in front of her at dinner time (occasionally she doesn't want to eat that either). Before bed, we select a few books from the foot-tall stack of children's books that I constantly keep in rotation from the library. Then she goes to bed (immediately on good days, extremely slowly on challenging days).

This environment and routine prime her for growth. If you or I were being cared for in the same way, our minds would be growing at a pretty amazing speed as well.

Out of the entire list of extensive routines, I believe the most important one is going to school. This provides Rosie with a learning program and a teacher.

Think about the time when you were in school. The one thing that you didn't have to worry about when in school was lessons planning. You know that if you listen to the lectures, do the homework, and practice for exams, you will most likely achieve the learning objectives set out at the beginning of the course.

The other way to challenge yourself is just jump in. "I feel like I am always on the bleeding edge of my ability," says Ashlee, entrepreneur and mom of two.

"The more we embrace not knowing and mistakes and

struggles, the more we set the stage for growth, success, and achievement," said Dr. Becky Kennedy, the author of *Good Inside*. "And this is true for adults and kids alike, and it's a critical reminder about the importance of normalizing difficulties, embarrassing mistakes as an opportunity to learn, and building frustration tolerance."

The Not-for-Profit Experiment

Shortly after my daughter was born, I noticed a very specific emotional change—I could no longer stand the idea of children suffering. All of a sudden, I felt true emotional pain whenever I heard about anything bad happening to a child.

That year, 2019, India experienced one of its largest monsoons in decades. The series of floods spread over many states, and over fifteen hundred people died. When I saw the news, it was accompanied by a photo of a man trying to evacuate his flooded home. Under his arm were a pair of small legs, showing the child he was carrying while wading through the heavy brown water.

The image broke my heart.

When I got home, I made a donation to the Red Cross for the disaster relief effort. But that didn't seem enough; my mind just couldn't be quieted: that pair of tiny legs could have been my daughter's. This was a terrible thing to happen to any family. I must do more.

"I'm starting a nonprofit," I said to Jeff.

We'd been married for a few years at this point, and he had gotten used to my sudden non sequiturs.

"Sure," he said. "What's the name going to be?"

I thought for a minute and replied, "Saving Babies from Natural Disasters."

"Descriptive," he responded. "But it's a bit limiting, don't you think? Just babies? And just natural disasters?"

My newly fragile empathy was strongly attuned to children, so I decided to keep this new nonprofit focused on babies. However, he was right, it shouldn't be just limited to natural disasters. Therefore, I changed the name to Saving Babies from Natural Disasters and Other Disasters Too (a nod to *Zoolander*).

Armed with only a very vague notion and a ridiculously long but descriptive name, I started talking to close friends about my nonprofit idea. Donating to the Red Cross didn't seem impactful enough, I explained. I wanted to give the money to that man in the photo. I wanted to make sure that child was alright. With today's technology, it should be possible for a donor to track down a specific recipient, for the donor to give directly to the recipient, and for the transaction to be both legal and tax deductible.

The more I talked about it, the more I was able to refine my thoughts. At this point, I began reaching out to friends and acquaintances through emails and short meetings. I have this nonprofit idea I explained; it needs refining, but I think it is feasible. The two people who responded enthusiastically were Sophia and Princess. I adore these ladies. They are both kind-hearted and go-getters, and I would love collaborating with them any day.

After just a few more conversations, we had a path forward: we needed to learn how to run a nonprofit and figure out how to directly connect donors and recipients. The three of us would meet each week to brainstorm, come up with doable steps (specific actions that can be done within just one to two hours), regroup the next week, and repeat.

I know of this small NGO, Armor of Hope Ministries, that's been doing good work in the village of El Sauce, Honduras, for years. Its founder, Laura Ross, started traveling to El Sauce a few months each year to provide nursing services. Slowly she built up community trust in Honduras and a donation base in the States. By the time I was introduced to Laura in 2018, her NGO had built a clinic, a school, and a nursing home in the community.

I contacted Laura, asking if she would be willing to share her experience and coach us along the way. Laura was spending six months in Honduras each year, but she said she was happy to help when she was in the States and didn't have to talk using an expensive satellite phone.

Even though we had to give up looking for that child in the photo (neither the man nor the child's face is visible), there are definitely thousands of children who could benefit equally from a donation. Sophia, Princess, and I decided that we could build up a backlog of ongoing work that is being done by amazing people—such as the clinic expansion project in Honduras that I learned Laura's team was doing—and use that backlog whenever we have trouble connecting donors to their specific recipient.

Week by week, we made progress and pivoted when we met with setbacks. Within a few months, we had a registered 501(c)(3) and began directing funds toward those in need. After a year of working together, Sophia, Princess, and I got together to take stock of where we were. Our biggest challenge was moving money across countries. There is a thin line between providing aid and money laundering. So far, we were able to avoid this issue by piggy-backing off of existing NGOs' established channels. In order to build our own channel, we would need professional help. This meant either finding some big-hearted lawyers and accountants or diverting our funds toward overhead. This was something I was adamantly against—I wanted 100 percent of donors' money going to the recipients and to use volunteers only. If we compromised on that principle, then our work essentially boiled down to creating a list of reputable nonprofits for donors.

Sophia, Princess, and I agreed to terminate our 501(c)(3) organization. At this time, our own energy would be better spent on other endeavors. In the end, Saving Babies from Natural Disasters and Other Disasters Too did not win grants from the Bill & Melinda Gates Foundation, nor were any of its founders nominated for the Nobel Peace Prize, but we had a great time working together and gained valuable experience.

A Walk Will Do You Good

In 1920, British mystery novelist Agatha Christie introduced a fictional sleuth named Hercule Poirot in a novel called *The Mysterious Affair at Styles*. The character of Hercule Poirot is best known for his egg-shaped head and his meticulously groomed large walrus mustache. He has appeared in thirty-three novels and fifty-one short stories, and I have read almost all of them. He now resides permanently in my mind.

Whenever I feel overwhelmed and stressed, I take a walk outside. There is a nice, shaded path close to my house. As soon as I step foot on the path, Hercule Poirot would appear next to me, neatly dressed, and say to me, "*Mon cher*, tell your troubles to Papa Poirot." And I would. Together, Poirot and I would take several turns around the path, me realistically and actually, Poirot imaginarily, and I would offload my mind and heart. Poirot, living in my head, would murmur appropriate words, such as "*en effet*" or "*eh bien*" or "*mais oui*" at the appropriate moments (the entirety of my very limited French is from Christie's novels). At the end of our walk, Poirot would always implore me to leave my troubles with him and believe that all will be well.

For over ten years, I've taken walks with Poirot, and he's never been wrong—all has always turned out well.

Cal Newport, Georgetown professor and author of *Deep Work: Rules for Focused Success in a Distracted World*, describes his walking routine as productive meditation.

"The goal of productive meditation is to take a period in which you're occupied physically but not mentally—walking, jogging, driving, showering—and focus your attention on a single well-defined professional problem," described Newport. "[Productive meditation] has the ability to rapidly improve your ability to think deeply.[2]

Whether you decide to talk to Sherlock Holmes, or go all the way to the top like Sansone, the key is to make it a habit and truly, actually, deeply believe.

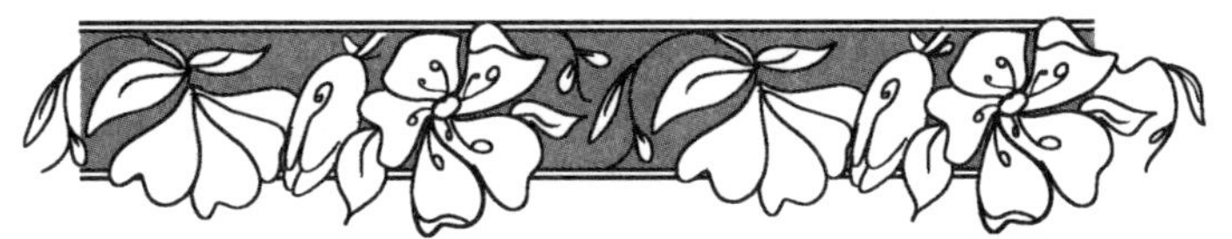

CHAPTER 11

Enough, Enough, Enough

Many people believe motherhood is about nurturing children with a lot of sacrifice on the mother's part. While certain lifestyle changes are inevitable, I do not believe sacrifice should be the center of a mother's life.

I wrote this book, not because you're not enough, but because you can have so much more without sacrificing it all to raise healthy and happy children.

This book first asked you to dream big. To remember a time when everything was possible, and you can ask for the world. Once you know what you want, this book can guide you toward strategies to get more resources in your life to self actualize.

Time, money, energy, and space are things all mothers can use more of. We explored ways to gain more in each of these aspects:

- **Time**—Using a combination of the Pareto Principle and "Good Enough Is Perfect" could get you about 80 percent of your time back. Whatever you choose to do in that time is up to you—without the guilt.
- **Money**—We need to spend money; there's no way around that. However, we can save money by avoiding predatory marketing that promises us that their products will make us better parents or make our children more successful. It's easy to presume that every dollar spent on your child is a dollar well spent but your child will benefit far more from your attention.
- **Energy**—Part of self-actualizing your dreams is to have the energy to get there. Together, we customized science and research to come up with your personal energy level. As we patiently respect our limits, we can find the extra bits of natural energy we need to take care of ourselves and others.
- **Space**—I explained how your to-do list might take up unwanted space in your head (and drain your energy too). Once you download everything from your head to paper, your mind will clear up, providing you with the space you need to dream even more.

I wrote this book because I have so much love and respect for you. The work you do every day to make sure your home and family are running properly, plus any other job or project you take on, is invaluable.

I could see that mothers face hardships—some passed down through society or our families. It's truly unfair and often feels unescapable. While I can't wipe away generational trauma, mounting hospital bills, and incessant crying, I found I could do something for us. This book pinned problems down like a high school biology project so we can see the root of our challenges and find solutions that truly serve as a win-win.

At the root of time, money, energy, and space is that feeling of inadequacy. With each generation, more and more is asked of women. And isn't it ironic that our kids aren't the ones demanding perfection—but our outdated expectations? Societies look to mothers to heal them but give them little time, money, energy, or space to do so. It's truly unfair to have this role thrust on us but feel set up for failure the moment we receive a positive pregnancy test.

You deserve the best this world and this life have to offer. We all do. And being a mother is only a part of it. You deserve to feel like what you have is more than enough for you, your children, your partner, and whoever else you share your life with. You already have what you need to be a mother and whoever else you dream of being. Together, we can calculate and tailor solutions for our households and throw all the other outdated expectations out.

Revisit these chapters whenever you need a reminder of just why motherhood expectations are so impossibly high. And revisit them to remember that you can, in many ways "have it all" if you want to—without just relying on wishing and a precious babysitter. I hope that these chapters will get you out of the worst mind spaces and into a future you want for yourself—not just your family.

Now, I urge you to go and hug your children, then start dreaming big and going after everything you've ever wished for. Remember, you got this. You always have.

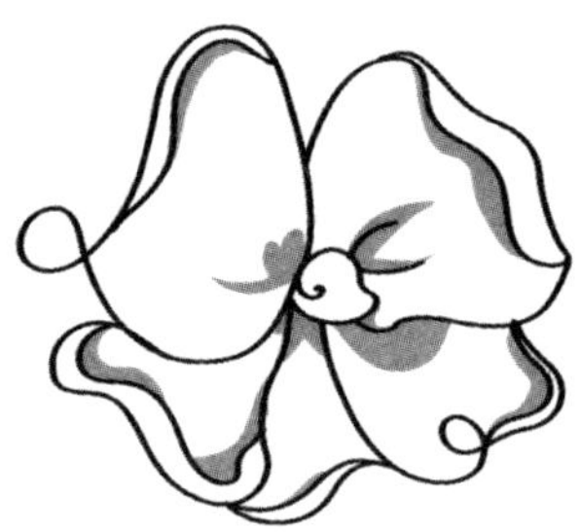

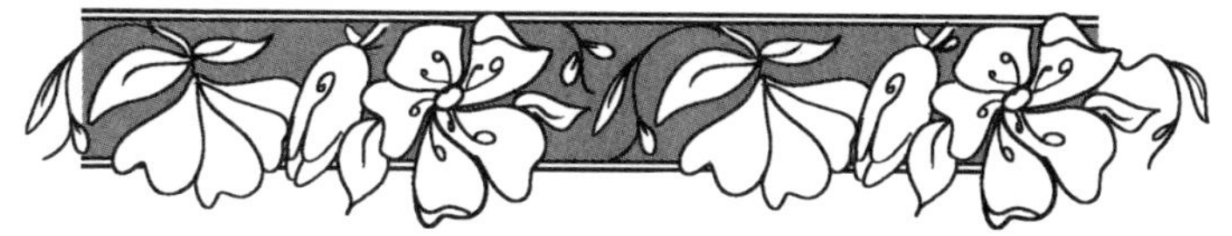

Epilogue

"You can't swoon every time you look at our daughter," my husband chuckled.

"How can you not? She's so CUTE!" I squealed in pure joy.

Our little family was at the playground. Rosie had decided that rocks are ice cream and was focused on creating the biggest sundae ever. It was dusk. We had finished dinner and wanted to get the last of our child's energy out for an easier bedtime, hopefully.

I would be returning to a messy home. We're still learning how to clean up to "Mommy's level of perfection." But what the heck, that's what the weekend is for, I suppose.

It's been two years since I started writing this book. I didn't realize what an undertaking this would be at the beginning; otherwise, I probably would have waited to be "ready" and never gotten started. As a foreigner to the United States and speaking English as my second language, I am extremely proud of this work, even though I can still find fault with every chapter. My goal is to encourage women to chase their dreams, however audacious, even at the busiest time of their lives.

After Rosie turned two, Jeff and I tried for another child. I had no difficulties conceiving the first time and my second try was no different. However, we lost the child very early in that pregnancy. I was due for my first ultrasound appointment the day I experienced massive bleeding. I called the doctor's office to let them know I wouldn't be coming in.

I was going to have another girl. I was going to name her Daisy. And she was going to be my second flower child. I didn't even get a chance to hear her heartbeat before she left me, and I was completely devastated.

We tried again, but when I lost the next pregnancy as well, I told Jeff *no more*. I could not bear to lose another child again, and we would just have to give all our love to our firstborn.

I finally got my promotion, two years after asking my manager for one. Throughout this book, I joked about being a slacker at work, but the truth is more complicated. Too often, I worked around the clock, putting in fourteen-hour days and putting out fires at work. I've had colleagues tell me that they would never want my job because of how demanding it looked.

It is demanding. There are days when I shut down my computer after 10:00 p.m., pull out a bottle of wine from the fridge, and commence revenge bedtime procrastination by watching *Bridgerton,* knowing full well that I would have to start back up the next day by 6:00 a.m. But I have an incredible team of people supporting me at work and a phenomenal husband supporting me at home. After each wave of challenge was dealt with, all I felt was a flush of pride at everything we accomplished together. And yes, there are also days when I spend too much time scrolling through the photo album on my phone and smiling at my daughter's pictures.

I now have another dream that I'm working toward instead of waiting for "the right time." I'm starting a publishing company.

I became absorbed with all aspects of books while writing this one. I read piles of other people's writing, worked with a number of talented yet patient editors, and met up with other writers (usually to commiserate about the lack of progress we're making on our manuscripts).

I especially loved connecting with children's book authors. To me, their writing felt like poetry: simple, playful, short, and sweet. I love reading their books to Rosie each night and eventually grew curious to learn more about the people whose words filled our nighttime routine.

It turned my curiosity into an obsession—tracking down children's book authors, asking them for autographs, attending their events, and interviewing them about their work. I learned that even though we are seeing many more diverse books today, behind the scenes, our authors still sensed there was an unspoken "quota" that publishers were sticking to. Only certain manuscripts were accepted, and only a certain number of those manuscripts were published.

"Nothing too spicy," was the way a LGBTQ+ author described it. "In fact, no jalapeño at all."

On the other hand, I can't get enough of those books, whatever flavor they come in. I want them all!

"This," I thought to myself, "is a market problem: plenty of demand with a faulty supply chain." Perhaps this is my chance to get into publishing too.

Not long after I had that thought, I signed up my first author. She is a professor at Howard University and already a seasoned author: a banned book, a bestseller, and several other works, she has appeared on the *Today Show* and *Good Morning America*. Why an author of such caliber would sign up with me, instead of staying with Random House, remains a happy mystery. But I believe if you keep your heart open, your dreams will find their way to reality.

Readers, if you learned anything from my story or research, I hope you learned that motherhood is challenging, but we have the tools and resilience to be the kind of parents and people we want to be. I hope that in spite of the social pressures and increasing expenses, you find ways to make your dreams a reality.

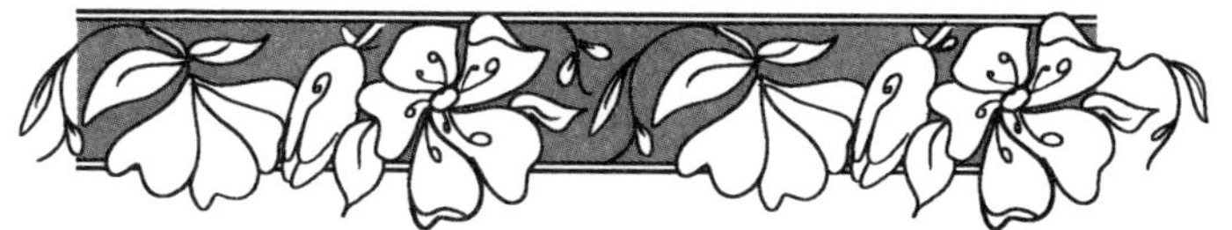

Notes

Chapter 1

1 Michelle J.K. Osterman, Brady E. Hamilton, Joyce A. Martin, Anne K. Driscoll, Claudia P. Valenzuela, "Births: Final Data for 2021", *National Vital Statistic Reports* 72, no. 1 (January 2023).

2 Kim, Pilyoung, Lane Strathearn, and James E. Swain, 2016. "The maternal brain and its plasticity in humans", *Hormones and Behavior*, 77:113-123.

3 The year of the Pig in Chinese zodiac, combined with "earth" in the five elements of nature (earth, metal, water, wood, and fire), creating the year of "earth-pig" or "Golden Pig" which occurs only once every sixty years.

4 Mays, Jeffery C. 2020. "1 in 5 Mothers Gets Postpartum Depression. New York City Plans to Help." *New York Times*, February 5, 2020, sec. New York. https://www.nytimes.com/2020/02/05/nyregion/postpartum-depression-treatment-nyc.html.

5 Henshaw C. 2003. "Mood disturbance in the early puerperium: a review." *Arch. Women's Mentl. Health* 6(2):S22-42.

6 *Annual Review of Medicine*, Postpartum Depression: Pathophysiology, Treatment, and Emerging Therapeutics, Annu. Rev. Med. 2019. 70:183-96, Stewart and Vigod.

7 Henshaw. "Mood disturbance."

Chapter 2

1 Larson, Erik. *The Splendid and the Vile: A Saga of Churchill, Family, and Defiance During the Blitz.* New York: Crown, 2020.

2 Podcast *Pivot*, episode 359, November 25, 2022.

3 Lee, Noel M., and Sumona Saha. "Nausea and Vomiting of Pregnancy." *Gastroenterology Clinics of North America* 40, no. 2 (2011): 309–34. https://doi.org/10.1016/j.gtc.2011.03.009.

4 John Hopkins Medicine. "4 Common Pregnancy Complications." Johns Hopkins Medicine, November 1, 2022. https://www.hopkinsmedicine.org/health/conditions-and-diseases/staying-healthy-during-pregnancy/4-common-pregnancy-complications.

5 John Hopkins Medicine. "Gestational Diabetes Mellitus (GDM)." John Hopkins Medicine, November 19, 2019.

6 March of Dimes. "Placenta Previa." March of Dimes, accessed on December 21, 2023. https://www.marchofdimes.org/find-support/topics/pregnancy/placenta-previa.

7 Bayrampour H, Kapoor A, Bunka M, et al. "The Risk of Relapse of Depression During Pregnancy After Discontinuation of Antidepressants: A Systematic Review and Meta-analysis." *J Clin Psychiatry* 81, no. 4 (2020):19r13134. DOI: 10.4088/JCP.19r13134.

Chapter 4

1 Hewlett, Sylvia Ann. "Executive Women and the Myth of Having It All." *Harvard Business Review*, April 2002. https://hbr.org/2002/04/executive-women-and-the-myth-of-having-it-all.

2 Vanderkam, Laura. *I Know How She Does It*. New York: Portfolio, 2017.

3 The LA Times wrote an article in 2013, the year Vanderkam started the Mosaic Project, titled "U.S. Birthrate Hit New Low in 2013 as Women Delayed Having Kids." Women were grouped into ages 20 to 24, 25 to 29, 30 to 34, 35 to 39 and 40 to 44. I'm choosing age 25

as the youngest marker, considering that the chances of women in the age group of 20 to 24 with babies probably aren't making $100,000 and therefore wouldn't qualify for Vanderkam's study.

Kaplan, Karen. "U.S. Birthrate Hit New Low in 2013 as Women Delayed Having Kids." *Los Angeles Times*, December 4, 2014. https://www.latimes.com/science/sciencenow/la-sci-sn-us-birth-rate-historic-low-20141203-story.html.

4 Inflation calculation was using the US Bureau of Labor Statistics calculator, measuring January of each of those years against September 2023 (the time of this writing).

5 Vanderkam. *I Know How She Does It.*

6 Hewlett. "Executive Women."

Chapter 5

1 Rich, Adrienne. *Of Woman Born*. New York: W. W. Norton & Company, Inc., 2021.

2 Phelan, Thomas. 2019. *The Manager Mom Epidemic: How Moms Got Stuck Doing Everything for Their Families and What They Can Do About It*. Naperville: Sourcebooks.

3 Slaughter, Anne-Marie. 2012. "Why Women Still Can't Have It All." *The Atlantic*, (July/August). https://www.theatlantic.com/magazine/archive/2012/07/why-women-still-cant-have-it-all/309020/.

4 A survey in 2023 by the Pew Research Center showed that 61 percent of jobs cannot be done from home.

Parker, Kim. 2023. "About a Third of U.S. Workers Who Can Work from Home Now Do So All the Time." Pew Research Center, March. https://www.pewresearch.org/short-reads/2023/03/30/about-a-third-of-us-workers-who-can-work-from-home-do-so-all-the-time/.

5 Vanderkam. *I Know How She Does It.*

6 U.S. Bureau of Labor Statistics. 2024. "Table B-2. Average weekly hours and overtime of all employees on private nonfarm payrolls by industry sector, seasonally adjusted." U.S. Bureau of Labor Statistics. Accessed January 05, 2024. https://www.bls.gov/news.release/empsit.t18.htm.

7 Robinson, John and Geoffrey Godbey. *Time for Life: The Surprising Ways Americans Use Their Time.* University Park, PA: Penn State University Press, 1997.

8 Vanderkam. *I Know How She Does It.*

9 Human Capital Cloud Transformation Team. "Digital & Hybrid Work Survey." Deloitte, April 2022. https://www2.deloitte.com/content/dam/Deloitte/be/Documents/technology/digital-and-hybrid-work-survey-report-spring-2022.pdf.

10 Dowling, Bonnie, Drew Goldstein, Michael Park, and Holly Price. "Hybrid work: Making It Fit With Your Diversity, Equity, and Inclusion Strategy." McKinsey & Company, April 20, 2022. https://www.mckinsey.com/capabilities/people-and-organizational-performance/our-insights/hybrid-work-making-it-fit-with-your-diversity-equity-and-inclusion-strategy.

11 Ferriss, Timothy. *The 4-Hour Workweek: Escape 9-5, Live Anywhere, and Join the New Rich.* New York City: Harmony, 2009.

12 Vanderkam. *I Know How She Does It.*

13 Koncius, Jura. "Marie Kondo's Life Is Messier Now—And She's Fine With It." *The Washington Post*, 2023. https://www.washingtonpost.com/home/2023/01/26/marie-kondo-kurashi-inner-calm/.

14 Vanderkam. *I Know How She Does It.*

15 Bureau of Labor Statistics. "American Time Use Survey—2022 Results." Bureau of Labor Statistics, June 22, 2023. https://www.bls.gov/news.release/pdf/atus.pdf.

Chapter 6

1 Lino, Mark, Kevin Kuczynski, Nestor Rodriguez, and TusaRebecca Schap. “Expenditures on Children by Families, 2015.” USDA, January 2017. https://fns-prod.azureedge.us/sites/default/files/resource-files/crc2015-march2017.pdf.

$9,330 to $9,930 average = $9,630

$12,350 to $13,900 average = $13,125

(13,125 - 9,630)/9,630 = 36%

2 US Bureau of Statistics inflation calculator. Inflation from December 2015 to November 2023.

$19,380 to $23,380 average = $21,380

($21,380 - $13,125)/$13,125 = 63%

($21,380 - $9,630) / $9,630 = 122%

3 CDC. “When, What, and How to Introduce Solid Foods.” Center for Disease Control and Prevention. June 27, 2023. https://www.cdc.gov/nutrition/infantandtoddlernutrition/foods-and-drinks/when-to-introduce-solid-foods.html.

4 CDC. “Infants (0-1 Year of Age).” Center for Disease Control and Prevention. November 29, 2021. https://www.cdc.gov/ncbddd/childdevelopment/positiveparenting/infants.html.

5 Lino, Kuczynski, Rodriguez, and Schap. “Expenditures on Children.”

6 Lambert, Jonathan. “Living Near Your Grandmother Has Evolutionary Benefits.” Goats and Soda. February 7, 2019. https://www.npr.org/sections/goatsandsoda/2019/02/07/692088371/living-near-your-grandmother-has-evolutionary-benefits.

7 Kaplan, Hillard, Kim Hill, Jane Lancaster, and A. Magdalena Hurtado. “A Theory of Human Life History Evolution: Diet, Intelligence, and Longevity.” *Evolutionary Anthropology* 9:156-85. https://doi.org/10.1002/1520-6505(2000)9:4<156::AID-EVAN5>3.0.CO;2-7.

8 Hawkes, K., J. F. O’Connell, and N. G. Blurton Jones. “Hadza Women’s Time Allocation, Offspring Provisioning, and the Evo-

lution of Long Postmenopausal Life Spans." *Current Anthropology* 38, no. 4 (Aug/Oct 1997). https://doi.org/10.1086/204646.

9 Tucker, Abigail. *Mom Genes: Inside the New Science of Our Ancient Maternal Instinct*. New York City: Gallery Books, 2021.

Chapter 7

1 Hanson, Melanie. "Average Cost of College & Tuition." EducationData.org. April 3, 2023. https://educationdata.org/average-cost-of-college.

2 Educational Data Initiative reported in 2023 that college tuition has been increasing at an average rate of 12% annually from 2010 to 2022. Melanie Hanson, "College Tuition Inflation Rate", Education Data Initiative, last updated August, 2023, https://educationdata.org/college-tuition-inflation-rate.

Finaid.org recommends using a rate of 8% a year when estimating tuition inflation.

"Tuition Inflation", finaid, accessed in April, 2024, https://finaid.org/savings/tuition-inflation/#:~:text=A%20good%20rule%20of%20thumb,college%20doubles%20every%20nine%20years.

In this calculation, we are using 8%. Although that is an underestimate based on the reported average increase, I believe parents can still find a suitable college for their kids if they aim their savings based on an 8% annual increase.

3 This is calculated using the standard future value formula of FV=PV(1+i)^n. While I don't include an explanation of the future value formula in this book, you can google it at your leisure.

If you would like to calculate this yourself, using different assumptions, you can plug in the following equation into an Excel spreadsheet: = today's tuition * (1 + college tuition inflation rate)^(age your child goes to college – child's current age)

Don't forget, you'll have to calculate this four times, assuming your child would be going to a four-year college. Increase the "age of your child goes to college" by 1 for each year.

4 McCormick, Douglas P. *Family Inc.: Using Business Principles to Maximize Your Family's Wealth*. New York City: Wiley, 2016.

Chapter 8

1 Waaler BA, Toska K. Fordøyelseskanalens store og vekslende behov for blodtilførsel [Digestive system's large and changing needs of blood supply]. *Tidsskr Nor Laegeforen*. 1999 Feb 20;119(5):664-6. Norwegian. PMID: 10095388.

2 District of Columbia Public Schools. "Family Guide to Kindergarten Readiness Standards." Office of Early Childhood Education. August 2010. https://dcps.dc.gov/sites/default/files/dc/sites/dcps/publication/attachments/DCPS-Early-Childhood-Parent_Guide_Final%20%281%29.pdf.

3 Karp, Harvey. *The Happiest Toddler on the Block: How to Eliminate Tantrums and Raise a Patient, Respectful, and Cooperative One- to Four-Year Old*. New York: Bantam, 2008.

4 Kennedy, Becky. *Good Inside: A Guide to Becoming the Parent You Want to Be*. New York: Harper, 2022.

Chapter 9

1 Manoochehri M. "Up to the Magical number Seven: An Evolutionary Perspective on the Capacity of Short Term Memory." Heliyon. 2021 May 3;7(5):e06955.

2 Knott, Sarah. *Mother Is a Verb: An Unconventional History. New York*: Sarah Crichton Books, 2019.

Chapter 10

1 Dweck, Carol S. *Mindset: The New Psychology of Success*. New York: Ballantine Books, 2007.

2 Newport, Cal. *Deep Work: Rules for Focused Success in a Distracted World*. New York: Grand Central Publishing, 2016.

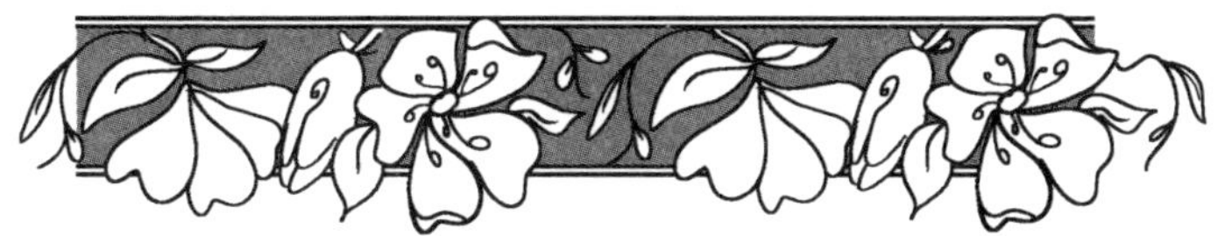

About the Author

Janet Bruins holds bachelor's degrees in electrical engineering and computer science from the University of Michigan and a master of science in engineering from Purdue University. With over fifteen years of experience as a professional engineer, she is a strong advocate for STEM education and global experience opportunities for young professionals. Janet mentored many engineering students, connecting them with underserved communities in Honduras, India, and the Philippines to address local climate change challenges.

The birth of her daughter sparked a transformative shift in Janet's life. Seeing the overwhelming focus on maternal responsibilities and the lack of personal fulfillment for mothers, she now dedicates herself to empowering women to pursue their aspirations. Cultivating personal growth and ambition among women has become her primary mission.

Janet also holds a master of business administration degree from Georgetown University and now works in corporate finance. She lives with her husband and daughter in Virginia.